The
New Single

ALSO BY TAMSEN FADAL

Why Hasn't He Called?

Why Hasn't He Proposed?

Don't Date Dumb

The New Single

Finding, Fixing, and
Falling Back in Love
with Yourself
After a Breakup
or Divorce

Tamsen Fadal

St. Martin's Griffin ⚑ New York

www.stmartins.com

The Library of Congress Cataloging-in-Publication Data is available upon request.

ISBN 978-1-250-06400-4 (trade paperback)
ISBN 978-1-4668-6919-6 (e-book)

St. Martin's Griffin books may be purchased for educational, business, or promotional use. For information on bulk purchases, please contact the Macmillan Corporate and Premium Sales Department at 1-800-221-7945, extension 5442, or write to specialmarkets@macmillan.com.

First Edition: June 2015

10 9 8 7 6 5 4 3 2 1

I AM DEDICATING THIS
BOOK TO MY DAD. THE MAN
WHO TAUGHT ME TRUE LOVE.
How to love, why to love, and why it's okay to love again.

I try to live his words and his faith daily so that they may

take me to the same place of happiness he has

known, including his life with my late mother

who never had the chance to

see me grow into a woman

I hope she would

be proud

of.

Contents

Contents

.Acknowledgments

Most of you know me as a TV journalist, author, entrepreneur, and host. Whether we have crossed paths in the studio or on the street or you have read my writings, you know that I have had a few bumps in the road. We all have. But it's what we do during the low points that determines how high we will rise in the end. I learned that a long time ago and it's been a lesson that continues to hold true year after year. For me, it started when I was young. I lost my mother the day after Christmas. I was twenty years old. She had always dreamed of a wedding, and me with a wonderful husband and beautiful family. But I hope she looks down, and is happy about how my life turned out despite what we had both dreamed of. I think of her daily in my journey, for the strength, the values, and the love she gave our family to handle life.

When I set out writing down my thoughts and what was working for me on a daily basis as I made my way into this new, uncharted territory of my life—my divorce—I had no idea that my random advice for myself would ever be published into another book. At first, I was simply writing down or keeping track of what worked to get me through my own breakup and the new issues that would arise daily. Only after spending time reading e-mails from, and talking to, so many other women across the country, in the same situation, did I realize it was not about divorce at all, it was about a time we were becoming a new type of woman.

I have so many people to thank, but I must start by thanking my dad, Jim Fadal, before all. He will forever be a believer in love. I watched him lose my mother to cancer, but go on to raise two kids on his own, and all the while, never give up on believing in love. He found Carol, years later, and to this day calls her his bride. He told me long ago that it is better to be alone than lonely with someone. He trusted in his heart and soul that true love exists and passed that message on to me, and I believe I can pass it on to you.

I must thank my brother, Cristan Fadal, and sister-in-law, Jenn Fadal, who listened to me each and every day of my then pending separation and eventual divorce.

My little brother was my rock, and the person who made me know that no matter what happened, it would all be okay and that I would come out stronger in the end. To my nephew, Sebastian, your little smile reminds me daily of the pure happiness in this world.

To my amazing editor, Elizabeth Beier of St. Martin's Press, little did I know that the day I met you to talk about my idea and thoughts, we would become true friends going through so much of this journey together. You have been incredible, and for that I will always be grateful. Your heart and soul and so much of your own advice to me fills up these pages and you made me believe that I could truly help the people who are reading this book today.

To Steve Cohen of St. Martin's Press, whom I met for lunch after years of trying to get together for an afternoon, on a very pivotal day in my life. A day that he helped make tolerable despite the fact he didn't even realize it at the time.

Carol Mann, my book agent, who met me over a decade ago, the first time, before I was even married. She encouraged me to put it all down on paper yet again after I was no longer married to share my experience and advice. She took my voice and took her experience to make this book possible.

Karen Kelly, from the bottom of my heart—thank you. You have been with me from the first time I ever thought about writing a book. You believed in my message and my voice and without you cultivating that voice, this book would not have been possible. You are the person I can call after months of not connecting and pick up just where we left off. Peter Goldberg, my TV agent who plucked me out of a TV market when I was just a cub reporter and made sure I believed in myself so that others would also believe in me.

Diane Danois, you have been my sister, my confidante, and the person who picks up the phone every time I need to laugh, cry, or ask you to repeat the same advice you have repeated a million times before. We met at a singles event in Philadelphia in 2001—and spent the night looking for guys. In the end, you were the best relationship that I walked away from there with.

Shannon Elizabeth, we may be cousins, but in you I have a true sister. You have been in my life in so many ways and I love every time we are together as a true family.

Beth Feldman and Marta Tracy, from New York City to LA you have both believed in me from the very beginning and have been with me to this day. I cannot imagine my life without your love, your encouragement, and your belief in my message. I love you both so very much. Rebecca Millman, a friend who has believed in me and continues to be someone who I can always count on.

To the calmest person I know, Jessica Bellucci. You took a lot of frantic phone calls from me over the years, and you have been the calm in so many of my storms. I thank you again and again—but it's never enough.

Christi and Ted Scofield, when I flash to all of the special times in my life in New York City, you have both been an integral part of those times from the very beginning. From advice to laughs to a lot of love that you both share with each other and the people around you. Ojinika Obiekwe, you are the picture of optimism by constantly reminding me to move onward and upward. Valerie Velez and Diane Pottinger, you both knew so much before anyone else did, and helped me feel beautiful inside and out—despite days that I didn't even want to get out of bed. Zack R. Smith, you have taught me how words can change a world and a person and a life. I am forever in awe of all those moments you turned into words simply because you listened and helped me explain myself in this book. You have all been true friends, never turned your backs on me, enjoyed me in the fun times and continue to stick by me even if there is a tearful night every now and then. I am eternally grateful for all of the heartfelt love you have given to me.

To the amazing women and men who shared their thoughts and stories with me. Your stories were so very personal and often difficult to tell. They are stories that helped me understand this is truly a journey and for each moment of it, no matter how difficult, we will come out on the other side in a better place and rediscover a better person in ourselves. Thank you for opening your hearts and trusting me at your most vulnerable times.

And to all the boys I've loved before, at the time I probably didn't want to say thank you—but now I do. You taught me it's okay to open my heart and it's okay if it just doesn't work out. It's simply okay. Thank you for the moments that we shared and the memories that still make me smile from time to time.

The past is a beautiful thing once you learn to live in the present.

Finally to Matsen, the furriest little man in my life that probably knows more stories about me than anyone in the world. He has shared more of my tears and my joy than I can ever remember. He licked those tears when I was sad or scared. He begged for pizza on many Saturday nights while we were tucked in a blanket on the couch watching movies. He gave me a reason to get up for a walk those mornings when I wanted to pull the covers back over my head and stay there all day.

Unconditional love. It's what I hope I give to you in the pages that follow. And it's what I hope you find a way to give yourself forever.

xo Tamsen

The
New Single

Introduction:
My Flawed Fairy Tale

*"It's better to be alone,
than lonely with someone."*

—DAD

In 2007, I was married in *The New York Times*.

In 2012, I was divorced in the *New York Post*.

Not exactly a Cinderella story, but it is my story. In this flawed fairy tale, Prince Charming and I ran a matchmaking business. A young couple, married and in love, helping other people find love. What could be more perfect? To top off the romance, we wrote two books together teaching women how to date. *Why Hasn't He Called?* was the first, followed by *Why Hasn't He Proposed?* When the story of our divorce hit the papers, the joke was that our third title should be *Why Didn't I Leave Sooner?* There were many nights that I asked myself that very question—but I wasn't laughing.

There are many things I learned from co-running a matchmaking business. *Everyone* wants to find *the one*. Everyone thinks about it, talks about it, dreams about it, and even pays for it—both literally and metaphorically. Most people are also willing to do just about whatever it takes to find and hold on to *the one*. If and when things go wrong, no one seems to know what to do next. You're not supposed to want to start over in your thirties, forties, or fifties, so the marriage experts don't usually put that part in the manual. I know we didn't.

Because my divorce played out in an embarrassingly, mortifyingly, nauseatingly public spectacle, I found that I had to take control of my suddenly single new life in a hurry. I had to learn that being a newly divorced woman brought out all sorts of craziness in myself, my friends, and in the men I eventually started dating. *Everyone* had advice for me. Some of it was quite good and some of it was simply dreadful. It was up to me to sift through endless, and sometimes hurtful, "suggestions" about how to live my new life and decide what made sense for me. I've written this book to share what I learned from others and my own experiences about starting over in the twenty-first century. I wrote this book especially because I came to understand the importance of regaining your emotional, intellectual, and physical wholeness if you want to successfully recover from a divorce.

Think about it. You were one-half of a couple before you were divorced. You saw yourself as a part of a larger whole, but that whole no longer exists. Who you become now is up to you. Will it be your own true fully actualized self, or a diminished version of the person you could and should be? I hope you will choose the former path, as I did. This book is here to help you along the way. I didn't tell most of my friends or any of my coworkers about my separation. I lost weight. I never slept. I wasn't myself. I cried a lot. I kept to myself. People thought I was upset because I was over forty and trying to have a baby. Little did they know the reason for my private anguish: the end of my marriage.

Then, I got Page Sixed.

In May 2012, the *New York Post* printed the first details of my divorce. Then came one article after another. If the first one was bad, the next few were rock bottom: details about our bickering and our blowups, my ex-husband's other alleged woman and, as Page Six put it, his other, other woman.

On one particularly painful night, I was master of ceremonies at a star-studded event. In between my hosting duties, and conversations with celebs I was bringing onstage that night, I was fielding e-mails and phone calls from the press while bawling my eyes out in the corner because I knew that more lurid, personal details were about to be made public. The next morning at the television station people were gathered around the newly delivered newspaper, reading about the lowest point of my life. It was understandable. It was shocking and unexpected to them. And because I had done such a good job of keeping my private life hidden, the details made public were that much more exciting to people, and devastating to me.

That's when I realized my marriage was not going to avoid being a statistic. After a lot of tears, fake smiles to cover the pain, rude questions from curious parties, and bank accounts that weren't nearly as balanced as they used to be—from mediators to separate apartments to the slashing in half of a once-shared business—I realized I had to face the fact that I was no longer a "we," and I was back to being just "me."

But who was I?

There hadn't been a "me" in a very long time. It had been years since I had functioned as a singular unit. Dinners, parties, holidays, even nights alone on the couch hadn't actually been nights alone. He had been there, even when I didn't necessarily want him to be. But having someone seemed easier than having no one. I had no idea how to be by myself. If only I had had an experienced, honest, and impartial voice to offer up advice about surviving this emotional train wreck.

Because I ran a matchmaking business in New York City,

I had no shortage of opinions about the single life, from both the male and female perspectives. I had clear proof that there were available guys out there, but in my post-divorce personal apocalypse, I had absolutely no interest in dating any of them. Instead, I chose to do what many women do following a breakup or divorce: I went back to an old flame. My first love, to be exact, and the polar opposite of my ex-husband: Professor Henry Higgins to my Eliza Doolittle. The man who taught me how to travel, cook, enjoy fine wine, and experience the world. The one that I thought "got away." The one that wouldn't commit to me when I was younger. And, as it turned out, the one who wouldn't commit to me later, either. Of course, Eliza outgrows Higgins, too. So, there I was, going to extremes, repeating one toxic pattern in order to avoid repeating another. This was not progress.

When I did finally start to date "new" men, because of my years in the matchmaking business, you would think that I would go out with nothing but Manhattan's most amazing bachelors. You would think. But, you would be wrong. For all the matches I had made, I knew what most of the people sitting across the table from me were made of, but I wasn't certain what *I* was made of anymore. Since then, I have spoken with countless women who felt the same way after their separations: disillusioned, and lost.

You name a twisted marriage scenario or dating nightmare, I've lived it. But haven't we all? From the stay-at-home mom who lost her husband to a younger woman, to Gwyneth Paltrow's "conscious uncoupling," whether we were publicly shamed or privately embarrassed, all of our stories are the same, even when all of our stories are unique. There are plenty of books out there about dating. I wrote a couple of them. This is not another one of those books.

When I was twenty-three years old, packing up my car and heading off to my first job in television news in Oak Hill, West Virginia, my father gave me some love advice. He told me, "It's better to be alone than lonely with someone." Quite frankly, the sentence made no sense to me. It wasn't until I was coming out of my divorce did I realize exactly what my father was talking about. I had been lonely with someone, but I had refused to see it. This book is about learning the difference and learning to cherish your own company. Only then do you even have a chance at being happy with someone else.

A breakup or a divorce changes you forever. You may wonder if holidays will ever be the same again. You hate the idea of dinner parties and being the odd woman out. You feel as though nobody enjoys your company—because *you* don't. The end result: another desperate night.

The New Single is everything you need to know about preparing yourself to be single again and getting ready for a new life, as well as a new relationship, should you decide you want one. These are the actions and attitudes that worked for me, day in and day out, and I want to share them with you. Maybe one or two sentences of this book will touch you; maybe you will sleep with it next to your bed stand and reread it over and over again. My hope is that you will understand that the worst is behind you, and that the future you create will be better than anything you experienced before.

Building a new future is a process, though, and, like any quality product, building it can take time. You will experience change in phases. Expect some rough patches early on, and some bumps in the road along the way. I never thought I would be successful at anything again after my breakup. In fact, despite my professional successes, I had never felt more like a failure. But with a lot of solid advice, a game plan and a change of mind and heart, I realized that this "ending" was a new beginning for the person I am really supposed to be. I want to help you find the same place. The only way you will fail is if you don't move forward from here. It doesn't mean you didn't have great memories or amazing moments that no one could ever understand or replace. It simply means you are in a new place in your life.

It used to be about him. Then it was about us. Now it's about YOU, and it's about time. Time to embrace your life immediately as the New Single.

This book is a road map for the journey from your breakup or divorce to your arrival at the place where you have become the person you are supposed to be. Or perhaps the person you were all along. What is contained between these covers is a pretty raw look at how I turned the end of my marriage into the life I was supposed to be living. I want the same for you. I've even put together a group of heavy hitters—experts on happiness, finance, organization, career, health, and more—to share their advice and insight on these and other important topics. Think of them as your personal A-Team, ready to help you through your rough patches and celebrate your successes.

Your personal journey to becoming the New Single will take about a year. Everyone heals and grows at a different pace. Which is why I'm not saying you have to do everything at once, but eventually you do have to do it. A year is not such a long time; make the most of it by not wasting precious minutes lamenting the past and worrying about the future. "Be here now," as Ram Dass would say. Do what you need to do when it feels right. I have set this book up in a progression, starting from what I think you need to do first, moving toward the culmination of you as a New Single: a secure, happy woman who dates but doesn't get caught up in the need to have a partner unless it's really right.

Some of my favorite books, the ones that I cherish year after year, have been the ones that I don't have to read from cover to cover. They are the ones that allow me to pick them up and open them at the times and moments that I need them most. I wrote *The New Single* so that you can pick it up and use it as encouragement to move forward. Or, break glass in case of emergency. I wrote *The New Single* so that you can grab it when you're asked the dreaded and inevitable question about why your relationship ended, or when you don't have a plus one for the party, or when you can't seem to lose that last ten pounds, especially before a hot first date. Thumb to the "*You* Are the Prize" section for a quick refresher course on how to make it the best date ever. This is truly the beginning. Embrace it. It only gets better from here, if you will let it.

CHAPTER ONE

Happily Single Comes Before Ever After

*"What a lovely surprise to finally discover
how unlonely being alone can be."*

—ELLEN BURSTYN

How Did We Get Here?

It was May 2012. One of those gorgeous Manhattan nights. Not too hot, not too cold. I was on the rooftop deck of the Gansevoort Hotel, attending a party for my network. You could see the city from every angle. As the sun began to go down it created a beautiful scene, a serene oasis in the hurricane of turmoil my life had become. Details of my divorce had just been splashed in the tabloids. I was not looking forward to facing the inevitable knowing glances, murmurs of sympathy, and, especially, nosy questions from my peers and concern from office friends, so I was hesitant about attending the event at all. Even so, I went. I had decided early on after my separation, I was going to try to say yes to everything.

I walked around the party with a chip on my shoulder. "I've got this," I kept telling myself. The articles had come and gone, and I was still standing, albeit on shaky legs. I was a newswoman and my divorce was yesterday's news. Onward and upward. I pumped my brain full of every generic bit of positivity I could muster, and shut away the sadness I was feeling. Then I looked up to see a former professional acquaintance standing in front of me looking like a slightly intoxicated grizzly bear.

We had known each other for a few years, though I was not particularly fond of him—nor he of me. In this environment, he was the last person I wanted to run into. I gave him that half smile that you give to someone whom you aren't in the mood to smile at, and said, "Hi." He didn't say a word. At six feet three—a tower of a man who, even at his most sober, stank of scotch and so often oozed the machismo of someone who had something to prove—he opened up his arms without a word and put them around me, crushing me to his chest. All he said was, "It won't be like this 365 days from now. Remember that." Out of all the sympathetic smiles and multiple murmurs of "I'm so sorry," his words were the ones that touched me the most. I remember them whenever I am trying to get beyond a new obstacle or a problem or another hurdle. "It won't be like this 365 days from now." While I still am not fond of this man, I remain forever grateful to him for his advice.

Trust Yourself First

It is important to know whom you can trust, but it's also important that you don't seek the advice from people who have competing interests, personal agendas, or on the other hand, are too kind to offer any criticism at all. My friends and family were way too nice. In fact, most of the people closest to me wanted to make me feel better, so they held their tongues when they should have just screamed at me about what they were seeing me do to myself. I found that it was important for me to have more than one sounding board as I was moving into my New Single status. My brother often kids around that I like to take polls to find out what to do when I have a dilemma in my life. Even as my marriage was coming to an end, I was constantly asking my closest circle of family and friends: "What should I do?" "Can I make this work?" "Will I be successful on my own?" "Was it my fault?"

I was lucky enough to have people who knew me very well and knew that I had a pattern of asking questions that only I could answer. I suggest as you move on and get past your breakup and evolve into a New Single that you look internally to answer these questions. Have people you can trust around you, but trust yourself first and foremost. Only you can get yourself to the next place that you are destined to be.

You Are Not Your Relationship Status

This sounds easy enough, but even in this amazingly advanced age we live in, the word "divorce" still makes people cringe. It's the way my grandparents used to refer to cancer—the *c* word. It's still the *d* word in so many circles, especially with the other *c* word—couples. A lot of people who are part of a couple don't love to hear about divorce. You can't blame them. I still don't love to hear about it, but this is about you and making sure your *d* doesn't define you.

The first time a friend of mine had to answer the relationship question on a form in the doctor's office, she froze. She had gone through her breakup and was telling me what to expect. "I couldn't bring myself to check the 'divorced' box," she recalls. "I wasn't the person I thought I was. I ran into the ladies' room and had a good cry." It's been years since Laura was in that doctor's office, and she's now part of a stable, happy couple, which helps her remember those early days of divorce with great fondness—that they are now behind her.

Remember this. You are not a classification. Single. Divorced. Widowed. You are not a statistic. You are someone who is about to embark on a whole new dynamic of your life and a whole new relationship with yourself. If you are not there yet, it's okay, but know that you will be. I remember the day my husband moved out of our apartment. Every single item in our once-shared space reminded me of an experience, a moment, a time that we were happy. In that moment I could not imagine being an "I" instead of a "we."

I had to take it one hour at a time and then one day at a time. In fact, to be quite honest, I refused to believe our separation and divorce were happening for a long time, not because we were so happy together, but because I was so afraid to be single again. It was important for me to realize that where I was two years ago was not where I was going to be today.

A-TEAM FEATURE   *Regaining Your Confidence*

My friend, Dr. Diana Kirschner, is a psychologist, a PBS love expert, and a best-selling author. She's helped thousands of singles and couples find the relationship of their dreams. Dr. Diana is the author of *Find Your Soulmate Online in Six Simple Steps; 30 Days to Love: The Ultimate Relationship Turnaround Guide; Sealing the Deal: The Love Mentor's Guide to Lasting*

Love, and the best-selling dating book *Love in 90 Days,* which is the basis for her one-woman PBS TV show, *Finding Your Own True Love.*

DEFINE YOUR CONCEPT OF CONFIDENCE.

Having a sense of self-worth, deservedness, and self-love so that you feel connected to others and attractive, lovable, loving, and successful as a person and as a woman.

WHAT ARE WAYS THAT LOW SELF-CONFIDENCE MANIFESTS ITSELF IN NEWLY DIVORCED/NEWLY SINGLE WOMEN?

Mourning for the relationship or longing for your ex.

Feelings of depression.

Loss of appetite.

Difficulties in concentrating.

Insomnia.

Aches and pains (physical and emotional).

Crying jags.

Loss of interest in usual activities.

Isolation from others (a BIG problem!).

Almost always negative self-talk about many or all of the following:

- Being too old, over the hill, too fat, unlovable, damaged goods, or unattractive

- Feeling bitter or untrusting of yourself.

- Self-pity, a feeling of victimhood.

- Judgments and resentments about all men being jerks.

- Loss of faith in people, in yourself, or in love.

These kinds of reactions are perfectly normal and not to be resisted or judged. It's all right to feel this way. But if you stay in these reactions you will hurt yourself by continuing a cycle of loneliness, low self-confidence, and low self-esteem. Women who hadn't gotten over a relationship by sixteen weeks after the breakup had decreased activity in brain regions associated with emotion, motivation, and attention. This is a physical change in the brain. That's why it is so hard to concentrate on anything—so hard to get up and go. Do not let yourself go this length of time without intervention (see below).

How do you rebuild confidence?

SHARING Talking about your negative feelings has been shown to lessen the activity in the pain-feeling part of the brain, and being with close friends causes the brain to release natural opioids, which are like the painkillers found in opium. A trusted friend can also boost your self-confidence. The same holds true for talking to a good therapist or relationship coach. If you need a coach who is an expert at helping women recover from a breakup you can find one at www.lovein90days.com/dating-coach/.

MEDITATION/RELAXATION Johns Hopkins researchers recommend practicing relaxation techniques to get rid of heartache. These include meditation, deep breathing, or journaling out your feelings. This process will speed the return of your self-confidence.

SLEEP is very important in helping to elevate mood. When you're depressed, however, sleep may be hard to come by. This is another reason to consider starting a regular relaxation or meditation program—these have been shown to help people sleep better. You can also try a warm bath with lavender oil and/or cutting off stimulating activities like checking e-mail, watching TV, or surfing the Web a few hours before bedtime.

EXERCISE releases opioids, those all-natural painkillers. Hitting the gym regularly can help you feel good about yourself. To start, just try ten minutes of walking, stretching, or any kind of physical exercise and see what happens. Those ten minutes can carry you forward in every way!

IMAGINARY CONVERSATIONS WITH YOUR EX People who have imaginary conversations with their partners, which help them to say good-bye, have more relief from grief than those who don't. You can write a letter you don't send or have a conversation with a pillow in a chair that represents your ex. You may want to do this in a session with your therapist or coach.

HOW CAN WE BUILD SELF-CONFIDENCE?

Here is my *180-Degree-Turn Exercise for Building Self Confidence*, excerpted from my new book, *The Diamond Self Secret: Say*

Goodbye to Your Inner Critic and Hello to Self-Acceptance, Serenity, and Lasting Love. It really works if you work it!

Read each section and then close your eyes, taking your time to do each step of the exercise.

1. Remember a time when you felt good about yourself— alive, real, attractive, connected, LOVING, and LOVABLE. You can go all the way back to some innocent time in your early childhood if you need to. Just find the most self-loving experience you ever had. Put yourself in the picture so that you are looking through your own eyes. Feel that completely.

2. Imagine yourself better, even better. Imagine yourself five times better.

3. Now take that image and bring it closer to you. Make it brighter, clearer. Give it a great sound track, magnify all those good feelings—make them stronger. This is what I call your self-loving Diamond Self (DS). Give this self a grand or playful nickname that includes your real name— like *Beloved Susan, Lovable Little Tami, Annie Adorable.* Have fun and give yourself permission to be outrageous with this! Say your self-loving DS name to yourself.

4. Shrink the image of your self-loving DS and make it as small as a real diamond. Then put that image aside.

5. Get an image of yourself at a time when you felt self-doubting, self-critical, anxious, undeserving, invisible, rejected, abandoned, or unlovable. When you were overrun with negative self-talk. This is your Disappointing Self.

6. Take your Diamond Self, make it the size of a hand grenade, and imagine throwing it right into the center of your Disappointing Self, watching it explode, and completely destroy the Disappointing Self.

7. Now, instant replay. Imagine your Disappointing Self, throw the Diamond Self grenade into the center, and blow the Disappointing Self up again.

8. Speed the whole thing up and do it several more times.

Do this powerful exercise until you cannot get a clear image of the Disappointing Self. You will be shocked at how it frees you from your suffering! Do a quick version of this process whenever you need to feel better or be more comfortable and at ease with yourself (the MOST IMPORTANT person) or get ready for a date or anything else that feels challenging. The bottom line is, no matter how bad you are feeling now you can recover from heartbreak, rebuild your confidence, and come back better than ever!

EXPLAIN THE DIFFERENCE BETWEEN BEING CONFIDENT AND BEING EGOTISTICAL AND SELF-CENTERED

When can we recognize we are indulging our egos instead of being confident and "outer directed" (when we are sad we may have a tendency to wallow, which is self-indulgent and not healthy).

Get Personal With Yourself

Chapter Four is devoted entirely to self-care, a critical element of surviving your divorce. At first I was not sure how personal I wanted to get in this area; as it turns out, it's important to get pretty personal. So bear with me. This is the time you are building a foundation. Whether you are relieved to be single again or you are devastated by the idea of being alone, this is not a time you can afford to let stress get the best of your health.

Yes, you will have sleepless nights. Yes, the sight of food may disgust you. Yes, you will skip your shower some days (I will admit to this one—only to you). There will be days when all you want to do is just stay in bed. Even the toughest of women out there, who wanted the divorce and were anxious to put the marriage behind them, feel this kind of stress from time to time.

WHEN YOU HAVE KIDS TO CONSIDER

Not only are you dealing with your own well-being, but your childrens' as well. You cannot take care of your children by neglecting yourself. You are no good to them if you are not whole yourself. This is a time that many children inadvertently learn to take care of themselves. They often grow responsible faster and learn that they, too, are individuals. So, be the best you can for yourself and for them, but try not to sacrifice either in the process. With those goals in mind, it leaves less time to mourn the loss of your breakup or divorce and gives you a clear purpose to forge ahead and make a new life for yourself.

Accept Your Life Is Different Now

As time went by, I realized that I was part of a community of single women who were successful in their careers and able to meet any challenge work threw at them, but they were perplexed about the next steps in their new personal lives. We all wondered about how to start dating again, how we would get beyond the breakup, and, most of all, how to gracefully and healthily move into this new phase of our lives. A woman I met through a networking group, Gina, who is the owner of a trendy Brooklyn clothing shop, put it: "I look like I'm ready to get back in the game, but I can't remember the rules." By this Gina meant not just dating, but participating in the little everyday rituals at work and out and about: water cooler chat about what happened last night, remembering to buy three ounces of ground beef instead of six— the little things.

I faced this dilemma by compartmentalizing my life so that my personal problems did not bleed over into my career. I was very careful talking with people about my divorce, including who was at fault, what my ex was doing now, or what I was doing. It's easy to get sucked into those conversations, and I caution against doing so. Don't talk about your ex at work. It is unprofessional and can snowball into unpleasant and harmful gossip. In fact, I could count on one hand the number of people I spoke to at work about my personal life.

At the water cooler I made it a point to keep the conversation about those around me, and not myself. I just didn't want to be in a position of wallowing in my own misery, or feeding off the pity of others. This was essential for peace of mind. At the time, I was waking up at 2 A.M. to be on the air at 4 A.M. for the news. I made sure the moment I hit the door at work,

I was not calling, texting my ex, talking to him, handling personal problems, scouring his social media pages, or asking anyone about him. Out of sight, out of mind, definitely worked for me.

TAMSEN'S TIPS   *How to Not Contact Your Ex*

---

1. Don't tell yourself you can just be friends. It is too soon.

2. Remember he won't give you closure. Only you can do that for yourself.

3. If he reaches out about the kids—of course that is a reason to talk.

4. If he reaches out about financial matters—leave that to your attorney or your mediator or answer the question and quickly move on.

5. Write down the "one more thing I have to tell him." Then throw the piece of paper away.

6. If he missed "his stuff," he would have taken it. Put it out of sight.

When I left the television studio each day, I made countless to-do lists that organized my time and helped me form new habits based on *my* needs, not the necessities of a couple. I know it sounds a little dopey, but the fact is those lists in the early days after my divorce kept me focused on learning to respect and meet the physical and emotional requirements of being the New Single.

Keep Your Breakup Out of the Places It Doesn't Belong

There are days your breakup or divorce is simply never going to be far from your mind. Yes, you will get through them and move on from there. There will be the moments you laugh about much later on, but this is a pivotal time in your life, and there are some days that will live with you forever. I am about to describe one of mine. It was the day I realized I was truly alone in New York City. I no longer had a partner and I was about to start over in the scariest place ever. BY MYSELF.

It's Better to Be Alone Than Lonely With Someone

When my father first gave me the advice in the header above, I was utterly confused. One of the major reasons we stay in unhealthy relationships is that we are afraid to be "alone." The idea of walking into a restaurant and having to approach the hostess with "Just one, please" is a daunting, terrifying, and depressing thought for many of us. It was for me.

The truth is that we are not afraid of physically being without someone, but that we are often afraid to be alone with our thoughts and our feelings. We are afraid of what we may discover about ourselves we don't like, or, worse yet, our fears and vulnerabilities will surface and we won't be able to cope with them. It's also true we convince ourselves that others, smug in their coupled state, are secretly laughing at or pitying our singleness, and are judging us.

My time alone was impossible at first. I would do anything not to be by myself simply because I believed I was not going to be able to deal with all of the thoughts and feelings I was working so hard to suppress. It took some work, but before long I realized that suppression wasn't working anyway, so it made no sense to worry about the inevitable.

It also helped me to turn to a close friend, Nancy, who had never married. She always seemed happy with her life, and certainly never missed a chance to see the latest movie or try the trendiest new restaurant. I asked her if she ever felt funny doing all the things I had thought of as "couples stuff" by herself. She gave me some incredibly helpful advice that I will pass on to you. But first she gave me a lecture: "Life is all about choices," Nancy said. "You have a choice: do you want to indulge your passion for foie gras and Chateau d'Yquem served by a hunky waiter, or do you want to sit home and make do with a liverwurst sandwich washed down by white zinfandel? Do you want to see *The Book of Mormon,* or watch a *Frasier* rerun for the forty-seventh time?" When she put it that way, the choices seemed pretty obvious.

Nancy's advice was as simple as it was direct: you are responsible for your own happiness. The couple at the next table is responsible for theirs. It does not matter the least to them if you are alone at your table, with someone, or at home. They are not paying attention to you. You have that privilege—and it is a privilege—so take advantage of it!

Nancy encouraged me to understand that "being alone" is not the same thing as being lonely, nor it is a disease from which one must be cured. In fact, being alone can open a whole new, exciting world. It allows you to start redefining your moments all over again. In my case, I began to travel to places I'd always wanted to visit, but my ex did not. In a very short period of time I went to Italy, France, Dubai, and back to Italy again. I don't know if it was necessarily my *Eat, Pray, Love* trip, but it was definitely exciting, it opened up a whole new way for me to think, and made me excited about the future.

I am a firm believer that you cannot and will not find the right person if you are not the right person already. You have to know who you are and what you want and what you need before you can ever find the person who will be right for you.

I learned that I didn't want to be with someone who isn't curious about the world. I love to learn. I can't wait to discover something new every day. I love to travel. In my marriage, I made very few trips. As a New Single, I have been filling up my passport as much as I can without apology. I will continue to do this, even when I find someone I want to share my days and nights with. Traveling grew me. It made me feel whole again. It gave me confidence. And, perhaps most important, it reminded me what I love to do and what made me Tamsen. Please find what makes you (FILL IN YOUR NAME). It will be the best gift you ever give yourself.

A-TEAM FEATURE   *Otherhood*

If you are single and do not have children or thought you were going to have them with your ex, this breakup can feel like a double loss. I spoke with Melanie Notkin, author of *Otherhood*. Her book is a great resource for women who expected love, marriage, and parenthood, but instead found themselves facing a different reality—no child of their own. I have known Melanie for years and asked her to share her advice.

WHERE DO YOU START THE ACCEPTANCE PROCESS OF BEING WITHOUT CHILDREN?

If one wants children and feels like her last chance has come and gone in the aftermath of her divorce, it can be devastating. It can be heartbreaking if the man led one on to believe motherhood would come, one day. But now you know he was never honest about that, even though you hoped and prayed and believed he would change his mind on parenthood. Perhaps you wanted the relationship to be secure before having children and, as much as you tried, the marriage or relationship failed and now you have neither.

    Here's what you need to know: regret is behind you. Life, and the man you will love next, is ahead of you If you stay in the past, thinking about what might have happened if things were different, or if you don't move forward from the present, stuck in indecision or despair, you'll never meet him, your next love, up ahead. He's there, waiting for you.

For most of us, especially those of us with siblings and married friends, kids are all around us. You cannot (and should not) attempt to appropriate your nieces and nephews, or your best friend's daughter, but you can certainly participate in their lives—share their joys, cluck over their sorrows, share little jokes with them.

And while time may be ticking, or if time for motherhood has run out, know that you have chosen to find love again. And how that love manifests itself, when it manifests itself, and with whom, will help determine what happens next.

How to address the question—"do you still want to have children?"—especially when you are a little older

The first thing to do is answer the question for yourself. Maybe the truth is that no, you no longer want children. You did when you were part of a couple, younger, able to conceive with relative ease and, most important, able to provide your child with a stable and loving two-parent family. You are not part of a couple now, and you may be past the point where conception happens naturally or if it happens at all. Life does not always happen the way we expect.

When others ask you this question, how you answer depends on how you feel toward them. You might bawl your eyes out to a close friend as you pour out your disappointment, or you might simply shrug and change the subject if somebody else asks you. You are under no obligation to answer *any* question from a nosy acquaintance, no matter how "well-meaning" she seems to be.

Eat, Pray, and Unplug

About a year before my separation, *Eat, Pray, Love* came out in theaters. I knew what the book was about, but at the time it was published, it didn't really apply to me. Fast-forward to August 2010, when the film version hit the big screen, and suddenly things had changed. It was difficult for me to watch the movie. I had not reached a place of acceptance at that point. I do remember, though, Julia Roberts on her knees at the beginning of the movie, delivering her poignant soliloquy: "I'm in serious trouble. I don't know what to do. I need an answer. Please tell me what to do. Tell me what to do and I'll do it." To this day that scene strikes a chord in my heart.

Julia's words are words that I had said often by then. They are words I continued to say months later. The similarities ended there. I did not have the time for a yearlong sabbatical to find myself. I ate, but truthfully had very little appetite.

What I *did* do was learn to unplug—for an hour at a time. As a social media lover and a tech geek, this was not easy; yes even an hour can be difficult. But it was something that allowed me to just sit in silence. It's okay to just be still, to unplug and enjoy yourself. You are going to be with you for a long time, and the sooner you get to know yourself the better off you are. If you are going to be moving forward with renewed energy and strength and clarity for a restart on life as you knew it yesterday, I found that to unplug helped me tremendously. It allowed me to be still and it allowed me to look around at what I like to do: read, walk, explore, organize, and most important, have some quiet time to get ready for new challenges. Once you know who you are, you will know what you can and cannot accept for the future.

"A journey is over when the destination is reached. And that is how it works even in relationships. Two people come together and co-create an experience. They learn from each other and become each other's lessons. Once the lessons have been learned, the relationship dissolves. The soul contract is over. There is grief here because of the transition and that is the invitation for both to move to the next level in their spiritual evolution."

Uma Girish, grief guide, certified
dream coach, and author

CHAPTER TWO

Survival Mode—The First Ninety Days

*"No good marriage has ever ended
in divorce. That would be sad. . . . But
that has happened zero times."*

—Louis C.K.

I t doesn't matter if it was his fault.

It doesn't matter if it was your fault.

Regrets and doubts and "if onlys" just don't matter.

It's over and time to move on. But how? Where? These are the questions that are the most daunting in the months after a divorce.

I like the at-a-glance clarity that flowcharts, diagrams, time-tables, and numbers provide. A recent study found that in the United States, the divorce rate for a first marriage is close to 53 percent. The divorce rate for a second marriage is 60 percent. The divorce rate for a third marriage is 73 percent. When I looked back over the first year after my divorce, I realized that those 365 days divided themselves into roughly four phases, or ninety-day increments. This chapter is devoted to the worst of those phases, the first ninety days. This is the time when each passing hour can feel like a hellish mix of emotions, doubts, and questions.

Why do so many people consider being single such a bad thing? Is it because you are lonely at night? Is it because all of your friends are dating? Because you really loved the person you were with and you cannot imagine life without him? Or because our society assumes that adults must be part of a couple, and anyone who doesn't conform is a weirdo or a loser? I won't lie to you: there are a lot of folks out there who believe that. So what? My life is pretty amazing these days. It took some time, but the truth is that I answer to myself. I know what I am looking for and I am confident in my ability to take care of myself day in and day out.

Though initially, as I have said, I was afraid of being single because it represented such a huge change in my life. Change, even good change, is a little scary, and does not get easier when we age. *Of course* you are not going to like going it alone. At first. Read the quote at the top of the chapter: "No good marriage has ever ended in divorce." You are here now and you need to move forward to survive the first ninety days.

As I was thinking about this book, I was trying to figure out what to compare a breakup to: an earthquake, a hurricane, a rainstorm, or a crash of some sort? Then it came to me: a breakup is like being lost; lost and not sure where to go, who to go to or how to start finding your way back.

When I was seven years old, I went to Sears with my parents. Shopping for a refrigerator, or a car battery, or jewelry, or khakis. Who knows what? Anything in the world of a department store can be overwhelming for a kid. Inevitably, something shiny caught my eye and I wandered off. Now, if you ever did this you, no doubt, have the memory forever burned into your brain. You remember turning around and not seeing your mom or dad. Heart-pounding, mind-racing, wild-eyed terror. I started moving frantically in any and every direction just to catch a glimpse of them. It felt like the end of the world and they had to be somewhere. Panic turned to tears. I was lost for what seemed like an eternity. Then, inevitably, my dad found me, and the world was right again.

After my separation, I sure wished that I could run back into my dad's arms so he could tell me it was going to be okay. That wasn't really an option, though, because dad can't be here all the time. It was up to me, just as it is up to you to make it right.

Be Still

Albert Einstein said life is like riding a bicycle. The way to keep your balance is to keep moving forward. While that is true, you're off the bicycle for a minute. So, catch your breath, and first stand still.

Through the matchmaking business, I would see a lot of people who had just ended a relationship and were eager to find another one. In other words, to get back on that bicycle. They were trying to avoid the lost feeling. Instead, they wanted to find a new person as soon as possible so that they would become unlost and back in the safe, familiar place of a relationship— *any* relationship. The problem is you will be lost until you find your new self. You cannot retreat, pull back, or avoid it.

Even if you were the person who outgrew your partner, it is important to stand still for a little while and figure out where you are and where you want to go next. Too many people jump into the next relationship only to find they are repeating the same toxic patterns or going the other direction altogether and finding someone completely the opposite of the person they were with or were married to. In my case, I did the latter and quickly learned that you cannot do that. As I mentioned earlier, I refound the person that I was once with and thought had changed. He was the polar opposite of my ex-husband, but he helped me sort out a lot of my thoughts. Through him, I remembered what I loved about my life and myself. I don't regret the time, but realize now that I needed to find me—by myself—first. It is not easy, but it is essential to stand still. Figure out who you are and where you are going.

As a woman who wants everything in its proper place, I am forever working to make sure that things get done, and done right. Sometimes, though, there is nothing to do *but* do nothing. Have you ever had a situation where you were trying to look up something online, got frustrated, and the minute you decided to give up and click to the next screen, the screen you were waiting for came up, but you lost it because you could not wait one second longer? Don't always try to click to the next screen. Give things a second or a minute or a day to sit and it will happen for you in time. Sometimes you get farther and farther away from the goal by desperately trying to inch toward it.

Survey Your Surroundings

One of the guys I met after my divorce had sort of a hipster quality about him. He always wore a necklace, a leather strap with a little silver elephant on it. Not a Republican symbol, but a Hindu deity. He really liked the idea of Ganesha, the multiarmed elephant known as the god of beginnings and the remover of obstacles. I didn't wind up keeping the guy, but I kept the symbol he introduced me to. I like that phrase, "remover of obstacles," because whether you are Hindu or Baptist or agnostic, we all have obstacles that need removing.

"Be the architect of your life and start building from the inside."

—The New Single

Remove the Obstacles

Your home is the place to begin. Just like your heart, your home requires a fresh start. Maybe you want to consider curbing the furniture you bought together (don't chuck it—sell it on Craigslist or donate it to Goodwill). One of the first things I did was get a new bed. My marriage wasn't exactly a Greek tragedy, even though it felt like it sometimes. In the ancient Greek poem "The Odyssey," the wedding bed was immovable, a metaphor for an unshakable foundation of love. It symbolized the constancy and strength of the marriage between Odysseus and Penelope. In the Fadal home, that sucker had to go.

I love my new bed. My old bed was dark brown wood. It felt heavy after my divorce. It felt dark. It was a king. My new bed is a queen. It feels light and airy. It represents the person I am today.

If replacing your entire bedroom isn't in your budget, or if you adore the furniture, make some small changes: new sheets and pillows, a new comforter, some new art. Make it a priority to transform your bedroom into your boudoir—a retreat that fulfills your innermost sense of style. From the bedroom to the living room, re–feng shui your living space. Turn your couch to face a different direction. Add flowers—a new scent. Get a new painting or hang some old photographs. Remember what I said about running back to my father so he could tell me it was all going to be okay? I framed and hung some of his old drawings in my home. They reminded me that my past was a happy one, and that my current sadness was a small bump in an otherwise good life.

As you re-create your home, take the opportunity to remove the things that may have once held meaning for the coupled you but that are now merely obstacles in the path you're blazing for the new you. Get rid of that sweater you hate but kept around because he liked it. Dump the loathsome Scotch he sipped but you couldn't stand the smell of. Make room for new things— your things. Clean out your closet and your refrigerator, and then take yourself shopping. Treat yourself. These symbolic changes will help prepare you for the emotional changes that will come in time.

When a colleague I'll call Lisa divorced her husband of fifteen years, he left behind furniture they had bought together but actually reflected his taste: clubby leather sofa and chairs, Mission-era tables and bookcases, and dark red and blue carpets. All perfectly serviceable and certainly authentic and good quality, but not only did the stuff remind Lisa of her ex, the colors and textures were dark and oppressive. She felt as though her living room was closing in on her. "Even after a great day out with friends, or a productive day at work, any high spirits I had would plunge immediately when I walked through my front door," she told me.

Lisa contacted a local auction house, which was more than happy to take the furnishings off her hands. "Let me tell you, it was extremely gratifying to sit in the back of the auction gallery and watch each piece sold to the highest bidder. It was cathartic."

She used the proceeds to choose mid-century modern furniture, which was streamlined and light. She kept the spaces in her once over-stuffed home uncluttered and open, while still adding many personal touches such as family photos, artwork, and mementos to the mix.

The putty walls of her apartment were painted a fresher gray-blue. Heavy drapes were replaced with sheers and linen shades. "Now when I walk into my apartment, it feels like 'me'— it's an optimistic place and now, even after a rough day at the office, it lifts my spirits." These emotions are not surprising. A new field of design and psychology, called neuroarchitecture, explores the impact light, space, and aesthetics have on our mood. Neuroarchitecture experts say when you walk into a room and see evidence of who you really are, you feel grounded— and happier.

Take a Good Look in the Mirror

Cue the Michael Jackson music because, "If you want to make the world a better place, take a look at yourself and then make a change." Seriously, do you like the look of the person who's looking back at you? If you do, that's awesome. If you don't, then welcome to the club.

People are shape-shifters, depending on their comfort or discomfort levels. I knew a couple whose bodies changed with the phases of their eventually failed marriage. When they got married, they were both in great condition. When she got comfortable, she put on twenty pounds. He stayed in shape. When the marriage started to fail, she got into great shape, and he plumped up. Obviously, the opposite happens a lot of times, too. In any case, at least one person usually comes out of a breakup looking broken. If you are that person, pay attention to what needs fixing.

Whether you're still svelte and sexy or not, you absolutely want to get your body in motion. Exercising cleans up your appearance on the outside and cleans out the way you feel on the inside. It's simple science. Exercise and endorphin release are linked to releasing stress and feelings of happiness.

I do yoga almost every day. It makes me happy. Maybe you need something a little more intense. Punch something, just not your ex. Boxing is a great form of exercise, and some of the most incredible and impressive physical transformations I've seen are thanks to some really aggressive workouts. You might also want to try Zumba. I dare you to leave one of those classes in a bad mood. Or maybe you want to make taking a walk part of your regular routine. It's physical activity and it's refreshing.

But you know that fantasy you have where you bump into your ex on the street and you're back at your college weight? That's all fine and good, but don't even think about a starvation diet. Bony and sickly isn't exactly a good look, anyway.

A lot has been written about whether women should get a new haircut after a breakup or divorce. Remember when reality TV star Kate Gosselin got those long extensions after she separated from Jon? Everybody talked about them—and her—and not always in the most flattering terms. But you know what? I bet that the extensions made Kate feel better about herself at a time when she needed a little boost of self-confidence that the new look provided. I, on the other hand, kept the same-old-same-old coif that I had before I even met my ex-husband. It's a style that works for me and especially for my job in front of the cameras. I say, if redoing your "'do" makes you feel like you've "washed that man right out of your hair," then go for it. If you have a style you love and that is part of your signature look, then hang on to it. It's about a positive self-image and projecting it from the inside out.

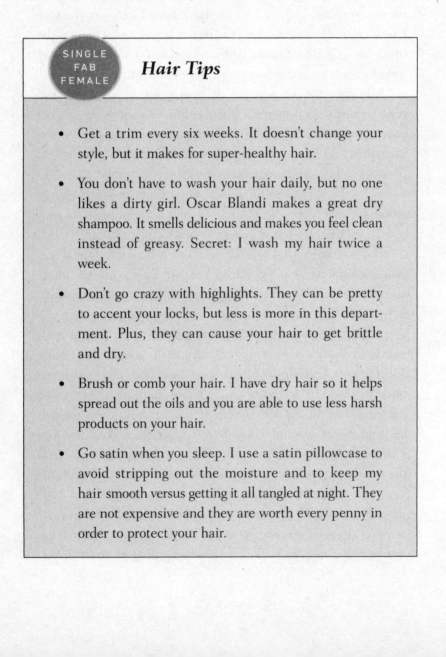

SINGLE FAB FEMALE

Hair Tips

- Get a trim every six weeks. It doesn't change your style, but it makes for super-healthy hair.

- You don't have to wash your hair daily, but no one likes a dirty girl. Oscar Blandi makes a great dry shampoo. It smells delicious and makes you feel clean instead of greasy. Secret: I wash my hair twice a week.

- Don't go crazy with highlights. They can be pretty to accent your locks, but less is more in this department. Plus, they can cause your hair to get brittle and dry.

- Brush or comb your hair. I have dry hair so it helps spread out the oils and you are able to use less harsh products on your hair.

- Go satin when you sleep. I use a satin pillowcase to avoid stripping out the moisture and to keep my hair smooth versus getting it all tangled at night. They are not expensive and they are worth every penny in order to protect your hair.

Take Inventory of Your Supplies

If you knew you would be camping in the wilderness for three months, you'd make plenty sure that you had everything you needed to survive those ninety days in the wild. The first ninety days after your separation are an emotional wilderness, and you need to prepare for the time you spend there. Take stock of your creature comforts, of the things that make you strong, and the things that make you vulnerable. Here's a checklist to get you started.

Stock Your Cupboard

Fill your fridge with healthy stuff—crisp veggies, healthy nuts, and beautiful berries that you can reach for when your energy is low (see pages 60–84 for more healthy single eating tips). If you love chocolate, buy the richest, darkest, most indulgent kind you can find. Even better? Look for the outrageously expensive imported stuff, so that you'll only have a small amount when emergency strikes.

If your routine includes a daily cocktail or glass of wine, have your favorite potion handy—in modest supply. Alcohol is both a depressant and an indirect stimulant, which means, if you're already down in the dumps, more than a couple of drinks will not only make you feel worse, they might very well encourage you to do something stupid. If you know that a couple of drinks will loosen your judgment, best stick to one drink and avoid the consequences of DWI, dialing while intoxicated. Better yet, reacquaint yourself with mineral water or seltzer and a wedge of lime on the rocks. They are healthier than booze, and you can sip as much as you want.

Adopt a Routine That Works for the New You

Susan, a woman I know who had been married for almost ten years when her marriage fell apart, spent three weeks every summer at Lake Placid. She and her husband rented the same cabin, at the same time, each year. When they went their separate ways, Susan decided schlepping hundreds of miles to rusticate for the better part of a month wasn't really how she wanted to spend her precious time off. She realized that what she'd loved most about the vacation spot was being near the water, so she spent many hours her first winter as a New Single researching different places to visit. Her only nonnegotiable criterion was "near the water." She settled on Martha's Vineyard: closer to home, surrounded by water and tons of restaurants, so she could spend her days at the beach, and look forward to a great meal at the end of the day. Today Susan credits her divorce with leading her to a place she now holds dear—but would never have found had she stuck to her old routine.

Plan Your Time

Susan swears that the hours she spent scouring Trip Advisor and Home Away searching for a vacation destination she could call her own helped her forget being alone and got her thinking about the future instead of ruminating on the past. I, too, found that if I planned my schedule and built in things I liked to do or a new adventure, I was the architect of the life I was building as a New Single.

Planning your time isn't just about planning vacations or

extended journeys. In the beginning of being newly single in particular, it's important to not leave yourself too much "empty space" and the opportunity to flounder and stay in bed with the covers over your head (and a gallon of ice cream on the nightstand). Both Susan and I, and other successful New Singles I know, would schedule enjoyable weekend activities—a brunch, a visit to a museum, a movie, walking with friends, so that when Saturday morning arrived we weren't stuck with that special kind of dread that comes with not knowing what to do with yourself. Yes, it's a distraction. But there's nothing wrong with distracting yourself if that's what it takes to get back on track. Psychologists have long believed that social interaction is one of the keys to moving forward after a breakup. Isolation, they say, leads to dark emotions that can cause us to think, say, and do things we will regret later—and which can prolong the recovery period.

Don't Panic If the Path Is Not Clear

Sometimes it's easier to do something—anything—rather than stand still. I know it is. Even now there are times I am simply moving around and keeping busy for the sake of feeling like I am doing something. It is exactly such times that you really need to evaluate. I have found that a lot of women make serious mistakes following their breakup not because they can't get over a guy, but because they are not sure what to do next and doing nothing feels like failure.

Some **common mistakes women make** following a breakup or divorce when they are trying to heal or just not sure what to do next:

1. Looking for closure in all the wrong places

"I need closure" is something we have all said. Just one more conversation. One more text. One more argument. No more "just one mores." Make a list of what you need to know. What you need to have closed. Then put the list away. In three months, you will look at it again and those things will look foreign to you. What is a ten on the panic chart today is usually nothing when you give it time.

2. Jumping into bed with someone

I am not telling you that you cannot be with someone. I am not telling you not to have casual relations. However, if you think that sleeping with someone new will bring back your confidence and make you a stronger woman, think again. Jumping into bed with some random person while you are in search of your self-worth does nothing but temporarily make you feel good—right before making you feel worse. Don't get me wrong, hooking up with someone new is all part of the post-breakup process—but at the right time. Until you have addressed your self-worth, try not to undress before you are ready.

3. Stop the small talk

And when I mean small talk, I am referring to talking ceaselessly about your ex with your sympathetic friends. What you did together (if you are not over him yet) or what he is doing with his life now (if you are over him) or why you haven't heard from him (if you are somewhere in between).

I had an amazing support system of friends who listened to me with patience and affection. They helped me through the worst of it, but there came a point when they had heard my various tales of woe so many times that all they could do was hope the best for me. I had exhausted even this most loyal group of people whose check-in calls to me eventually became less and less frequent. Fortunately, I got the message and kept my friends by retiring my repetitive "small talk."

4. Social media sweethearts

Move on. It's weird that at one point we didn't know what the words "social media" meant. Now, we live by them. So, hitting "unfriend" should not be as big a deal as we make of it. For a long time I just wanted to be on his Facebook page to "monitor" what was going on. Bad idea.

This is when we need to be clear with ourselves: no more living in the past. There is no relationship with him anymore. No more checking out his Vines, Tweets, Updates, Tumblr, Facebook, or any other kinds of update he has to offer. Unfriend. And click elsewhere.

LESSONS FROM SMART WOMEN
....

"You will never find the right person if you never let go of the wrong one."

—Unknown

CHAPTER THREE

Start Romanticizing the Future. Now.

*"The first recipe for happiness is:
avoid too lengthy meditation on the past."*

—ANDRÉ MAUROIS

The past is a funny thing. It defines all of us. It allows us amazing memories that can make us laugh or cry or learn. So it goes without saying that sometimes—oftentimes—you miss your past life. You romanticize it and fall in love with it all over again. The parties. The people. The holidays. The way it used to be was so great. It's sort of like a Gatsby complex. Nick Carraway said, "You can't repeat the past." "Why, of course you can," said Jay Gatsby. But that's simply denial, for Gatsby and for you.

The past wasn't as great as you remember it; otherwise, you wouldn't be in this situation. I am not saying to bury the past. It made you who you are. Every mistake you ever made brought you to this place. Just don't ruminate on it—it's really not worth your valuable time. Valuable insights from the past will come without you consciously thinking about them.

Stop Misremembering the Past

Leona Lewis sings "Better in Time," a song that speaks to me in so many ways, perhaps because it admits that time helps, but time doesn't heal all wounds. I wish it did. What time does do is allow you to figure out how to deal with the end of the relationship and the beginning of a new life. I spoke with a woman recently who shared that it had been three years since her divorce. She was no longer in love with her former husband, yet she would still become upset when she would hear about what was going on in his life. This time it was especially difficult. While on Facebook, she saw the news on her Timeline that he was getting married. As a result, she would spend hours looking at Facebook depictions of the other woman, her engagement ring, and at all the places the new couple visited. To her credit, in time, she wasn't "friends" with him on Facebook; however, due to "friends of friends" and other social media connections it's sometimes impossible to avoid getting information you don't want. In this case, she didn't want it—but she could not keep herself from looking at it.

She told me that after her initial hurt, and a flood of sadness and anger, she got very real with herself and remembered that the past was never as great as she remembered it. In fact, it was not very good at all. She had to be honest with herself about what was reality, instead of painting a picture of something that never really existed.

In my case, I have done the same thing and am still guilty of it, until I used what I learned through the grieving process and therapy to help me move forward the right way. To this day, when I get some "news" about my former husband's current life, I have to remind myself that when I was a part of it, it was certainly not the way I wanted to remember it. It is not easy to "shake the past," but it is necessary to prioritize it appropriately.

While writing this book, I went through the end of another relationship, one that I was in following my divorce. It was with a person whom I had memories with both from the past and the recent present. When I broke it off with this old "new" flame, the feelings of loss from my divorce came flooding back to me. Loss is never something we get used to. It is forever something we learn to deal with and learn from. But, if you walk away with nothing else, remember where you are today is not where you are going to be in one month, three months, or one year from now.

Each day I work to use my own words to make sure I am not living out a fantasy that is not there. I make sure (as difficult as it always is) to move forward. I make sure I don't paint a false picture of any ex. I stop taunting myself with photos, reminders, e-mails, and conversations about him. When you do those things, you keep that person very present in your life. Work hard to move aside all reminders of him. One day you won't have to do that, but do it while the wound is fresh. Let it heal.

"The past is a beautiful thing once you learn to live in the present."

—THE NEW SINGLE

It's Time to Be Honest With Yourself

When you are going through a divorce, it feels like you have to divorce not only your partner, but also your old self. WHY? This is the time to assess your life and get real with regard to what you want.

In my case, I had an amazing job, but I was so fixated on the breakup everything seemed blurry to me. Looking back, within a year of my divorce I had been promoted at work, I was hosting a new half-hour entertainment show about Broadway, and I was on top of the world in terms of amazing friends and a packed social calendar. How did this happen?

Answer: I continue to work on myself. No matter how good I may feel—there are the questions I make sure I ask myself and answer for myself as often as possible. These questions forced me to get real with myself, then forced me to streamline who I was, what I wanted, and where I wanted to be.

ARE YOU IN CONTROL OF YOUR EMOTIONS OR ARE YOUR EMOTIONS IN CONTROL OF YOU?

Choose control and choose happiness. If your emotions are in control of you, there is no chance you will able to focus on who you are and what you want to do. You must create boundaries (we will address this later in the book), and make sure that if you do feel emotional (and you will), you can figure out why you feel that way and determine an approach to work through it.

WHO IS THE LOVE OF YOUR LIFE?

You are. Don't forget that. It's not what society dictates or what the online dating sites tell you or if your family wants to "see you happy." You should be the love of your life so that you will always be open to letting love in.

How are you at your best? Single or in a relationship?

Think about how you feel when you start a new relationship. You are excited to get out of bed every morning. Why is that person so much better and different than your current state of Debbie Downer-ness? Just because you're single doesn't mean the sound track to your life has to include a sad-sounding trumpet (wah-wah). What makes you excited to wake up and start a new day? It's so important to **own your authenticity**. If the person you really, truly want to be is the person you are in the first stages of a relationship with, then there's no reason you can't feel just as full of life now. Because you are starting a new relationship, right now, with yourself. Own it.

Where do you see yourself in five years?

It's a classic job interview question, but it works for where we're going. Not just five years, though. Where do you want to see yourself in six months? One year? Three years? It's time to start living your life consciously and deliberately. And that means setting goals for the long term and the short term.

Those are the four questions that I work on all the time, and asking and answering them prepared me to get back out there in my career and my dating life and they keep me on track today.

LESSONS FROM SMART WOMEN

"Stay away from naysayers, men haters, people who don't believe in 'second chances' and negative people in general. If you expect and hope to find a positive partner, start by being a person with positive expectations. If love and romance is important to you and your life, keep showing up for it."
—Marta Tracy, television and media strategist

A-TEAM FEATURE

How to Improve Your Mood Immediately

I look for people who know how to inspire and encourage and really live their message. Jennifer Tuma-Young is one who does just that. As the author of *Balance Your Life, Balance the Scale* and a wellness coach, I turned to her to talk about how to find balance, healing, and tips to improve your mood starting today.

WHERE DO YOU START WITH FINDING BALANCE IN YOUR LIFE AFTER A DIFFICULT TIME?

Connect to Something Deeper—Whether it's morning prayer, meditation, or having a gratitude jar beside our bed, studies show that prayer and spirituality are among the best stress prevention and relief techniques. Not only will you be able to cope with a devastating situation better, your body will respond with faster healing, you will improve your immune system, and you will release less cortisol (cortisol wreaks havoc inside and out, so the less we release the better!).

Let's face it. Balance, in the form of having all of our ducks neatly in a row, is bunk!! Finding our anchor to keep us centered during life's inevitable ups and downs is key. An anchor is a core value—this is part of who we are and what we stand for. We all have anchors, but sometimes we get so caught up in life we forget, and that's perfectly okay! The beauty of imperfect situations lies in the gifts these situations leave us with—perhaps it is an opportunity for new awareness and self-discovery, a chance to grow in our faith. Being deeply connected to two to three core values is the best way to stay centered and anchored when life throws us off balance with curveballs! When we connect to something deeper, we feel more at peace, in balance, we experience real joy, and we also realize none of this is dependent on the stuff we have or the circumstances we are facing.

WHAT ARE FIVE STEPS YOU CAN TAKE TODAY TO IMPROVE YOUR MOOD IMMEDIATELY?

1. Do the Little Things—Ever heard the phrase "It's in the details"? This is so true for finding balance—it's not the "big" things that bring us balance, it's the everyday little things that create it! Finding balance isn't about being perfect, saying yes to everything, running around like a crazed superwoman . . . balance really is a state of being. And, being in balance opens us up to limitless possibilities, stronger relationships with ourselves and others, and all in all, living a joyful life. The details of life, like writing letters to loved ones, or playing an old-school game—charades, Scrabble,

Operation, Twister—bring so much joy. Sing in your shower, car, yard, or office, (bonus points if you sing loudly so others can hear you!), walk a neighbor's dog, cash in all of your old change and anonymously give it to someone who could use a little help. Change your bar of soap to something that smells fantastic, and really take note of the scent, breathe deep in the shower, and just be present. Relishing the little ordinary details of life makes it all extraordinary, and you will feel more in balance instantly!

2. Honor Your Physical Body—Yes, this means, simply put, exercising and fueling up on healthy food sources. When we honor the gift of our physical bodies, we are stronger inside and out, giving us a solid foundation to face the stressors life brings. We have a natural release of stress when we move more. There are lots of ways to connect with our physical selves—kickboxing works wonders, Zumba really gets that heart rate going, using machines helps you focus on breathing deeply (inhaling and exhaling), and for the non-traditional movers—climb a tree, bounce on a trampoline, swim in a lake—you get my drift. Jumping for joy is always good exercise, too!

3. Inject Fun and Play Into Life—While life can be filled with many twists and turns, ups and downs, injecting "play" is essential. Levity and laughter are not only fun, but both have proven to help prevent and relieve stress! So by looking at life through a lighter lens, it makes it easier to handle difficult situations. Adding creativity and lightness to situations creates a healthy environment for all those around you, as well as lowering the overall tension and stress levels of the group. You can begin by giving yourself permission to play, then naturally you will stop taking your-self so seriously—break out into a random dance party at home, sing loudly in your car, be open about your quirks, accept yourself (and others) for who you really are—and that is a magnificently made, amazing human being!

4. Serve Others—When life hands us lemons, it's an op-portunity to make others lemonade. Using our natural gifts, our natural abilities, to light up the lives of others, allows us to feel like we are contributing something to the world. According to the 2013 Health and Volunteering Study, volunteer work is just as helpful to the giver, as 78 percent of participants reported lower stress levels at the end of the study, and 94 percent said volunteering improved their mood! So, whether it's baking bread for your neighbor, smiling at a stranger, nurturing and nour-ishing your little ones, or volunteering for a local non-profit organization, helping others is healing to ourselves as well.

5. Be a Teacher and Be Open to Learning From Great Teachers—Teaching gives us a sense of purpose and value that naturally relieves stress because we are connecting with others on something we are truly passionate about! And, in our daily lives we are always teaching others just by our actions. There are lots of ways you can "teach" without necessarily being a teacher in a traditional classroom.

Live and Take Action—What do you want to teach? What would you like to learn? Take action on those things!! Sure, I can write about kindness and teach a class about kindness, but if I ignore the man holding the door for me to walk into the classroom, I am actually teaching coldness. Let your life be your lesson and your classroom, where you constantly learn and teach.

Join a Group, Network, or Organization—Share yourself, your life lessons, your mistakes, and your successes, with a support group or network. Share your knowledge and connect with others who have something to share with you as well. You can even offer to teach a class on a skill, passion, or hobby that would enrich the group and give you an opportunity to help others!

Be a Mentor—I am so grateful to the many mentors I've met in my lifetime—some knew they were mentoring me, while others just ended up being a great mentor by their actions and words. So, if an opportunity arises for you to mentor someone on something you've learned, share what you can with them— even if it's a few words of encouragement.

Be also careful to remember that teachers come in many forms, not just older, wiser people. Nature is a great teacher— learning from birds while soaring looks simple, but it takes a lot of work, even pain, to learn how to fly, and often that bird was kicked out of its nest by its mother. Children, precious gifts from God, can be our greatest teachers. They remind us every day of our essence, who we are each born to be. And what do they love the most? Sharing, listening, connecting, being present, looking at the moon and stars in the sky, telling a silly story, laughing, giggling, dancing, living . . .

Choose Happiness

When we are looking for happiness, often we look outside of ourselves to find it. It wasn't until I spent a lot of time studying what it was really about that I realized my true happiness was not in my perfect weight, the ultimate relationship, or more money. My true happiness is with me at all times. I carry it around inside of me. I make a decision to be. I make a choice to be happy. And as hard as it can be some days, choosing happiness is the way to heal and to be healthy.

You must be happy from the inside.

Yes, I get excited when I get a new pair of shoes, or my boss compliments me, or better yet, a surprise check comes in the mail. But the truth is, the real happiness is when I choose to be happy no matter what is happening around me externally. It is when I say: this is what I choose no matter how difficult the day is and no matter how much anxiety or fear I am experiencing at the moment. It is a conscious decision I make—to be happy.

Learn to access your inner happiness after a breakup or divorce.

I have learned that the only true happiness I get, that doesn't go away quickly, is when I put it out first. When I am a receiver, I am happy for just a short time. When I make people smile or feel good, not superficially but genuinely, it comes back to me. It comes back in a way that I feel on the inside and it comes back tenfold. I am my best when I am helping someone else. I am my best when I open myself up to love. And, I am my best when I am in tune with the world around me.

Tough Love

In my second book, *Why Hasn't He Proposed?* I wrote, "I believe that relationships are what matter in life." When I went back and reread that passage, I wondered if that still held true, for me personally, if not for all of us in general. In the end, I believe it does. Relationships *do* matter in life, none more than the relationship we have with ourselves. A breakup or divorce can badly damage that singular and important relationship, if you do not take care.

I really thought I knew myself when I got married. Maybe I did. But the person I know today is very different. A friend of mine wrote a letter to me not long ago to tell me he had watched me transition from single and happy to married and happy, then married and unhappy to divorced and unhappy and finally, back again to single and happy—and wiser.

Here is what he said: "For years, you slowly progressed towards darkness. You saw only failure in your life, and you gravitated to a long line of losers who might have been good enough as an acquaintance, but never your equal. I can't remember the last time you were with someone who was worth your time. During our last call, however short as it was, things were different. You saw success in your life and not failure; you had hope for the future; and you recognized that any time you spent with the wrong men was unhealthy and pointless (I didn't even have to say a thing about it). You reminded me of the kicking ass, taking names, version of yourself who knew what she wanted, knew how to get it, and would bury you if you got in her way. I've missed that girl for a long time, and I hope that as you come to accept that you're pretty damn special, you'll parole her from the bottomless pit in your psyche where you've been stashing her. You have taken your first (albeit small) step back into the light, and I think that's great."

When I read his e-mail I was shocked. Then shaking. Then so, so sad. Then . . . happy. The fact that I appeared to others as navigating my way through life under a dark cloud, always seeing only failure ahead was shocking to me, even though it absolutely reflected how I felt at the time. I just didn't think it was obvious to those around me. This place of darkness and failure was not where I wanted to be in one month, one year, or one decade from then.

So, I ask you: are you that kicking ass, taking names, version of yourself that you once knew? Do you miss her? Can you parole her from where you have been stashing her in your psyche? I sure hope you can. I hope that I can help.

On the road to getting to know yourself again, it's important to stay true to what you know. Did you love movies on a Sunday? Did you work out in the morning instead of the afternoon? Did you enjoy being alone? Is lifting weights your thing or is running or maybe Pilates? Do you love the theater or trendy restaurants where you can't hear anyone talking? Do you like to volunteer at an animal shelter instead of spending the day walking around the mall? It is so important to start doing the things that you used to like, but didn't do because your partner didn't want to do them.

I will give you an example of a man I was with for a while. He hated going out with anyone but me. No "couple friends." No parties. He wanted to eat early and in a quiet restaurant. He sounds like he might have been married to someone else, but he was single and selfish. I can't tell you the countless number of nights I sat at home with him watching documentaries (not that there is anything wrong with that, but I have to be in the mood). I slowly adjusted to our relationship, which isolated me—and him—from just about everybody else. He came from a family with a lot of money and was used to getting what he wanted. My family was not rich, and I have a personality that doesn't want to fight.

We were poster children for the un-perfect couple. In time, it simply didn't work. I grew resentful. So did he. The things I loved about him—his ability to have amazing conversations, his depth, and his calm demeanor—soon became everything I could not stand. When we finally parted ways, I was happy to resume my social life; I didn't spend every night, or even most nights, out on the town, but I also didn't shy away from the convivial company I have always enjoyed. Remember who you are. Remember what makes (INSERT YOUR NAME) feel whole. And then, don't let yourself forget it.

Looking back, my most favorite time post-divorce were Friday nights. I used to order a pizza and watch three movies in a row with my Chihuahua sitting on my lap. The key phrase: *by myself.* I don't sit still much. And as I mentioned earlier, I certainly didn't want to sit around doing nothing while getting to know someone new (those quieter moments in a relationship come with and in time), but alone time with yourself is different and important. I didn't realize just how important when I was at the start of my New Single journey. Initially, I was embarrassed to tell anyone at work the following Monday what I had done. I used to say I was running around, or that I didn't feel well, or friends were in town for the weekend. Anything but, "I stayed home by myself." After all, the New Single in New York City—what could be better than a Friday night? But once I started to embrace Fridays on my own, it felt good to know that I had enough confidence to do only what I wanted to. Make time for yourself a ritual. This is your time. Embrace every moment of this process as you break through. It will be the difference between big and huge strides in becoming who you are supposed to be.

Those Friday nights gave me to chance to relearn myself. I found out that I was okay with the TV on or off. I was okay with the silence, and it didn't make me want to cry. It was one small step that I was taking on the road to the next part of my life.

Eventually, I started to add friends to the mix, which was actually difficult because I didn't relish the thought of going out with couple friends that my ex and I had both shared—even just the women on their own made me sad. We address friends in another chapter, but for now, surround yourself with people who make you strong, not people who make you second-guess where you are in life. It is a very delicate time and you need to treat it as such. To this day, I walk every Sunday with one of the women my ex-husband and I used to be friends with when we were married. I don't think about him, and I cherish my friendship with both her and her husband.

Paint Your Past. Predict Your Future.

There are very few times I am ever going to ask you to paint a beautiful picture of your past and the things you loved about that relationship. In fact, this is going to be the *only* time I ask you to do it.

Things that you believe were so very wonderful you cannot

picture them out of your life. What we are attempting to do here is step outside of ourselves for a moment in a sort of Dickensian-McConaughian way. Did you ever read *A Christmas Carol*? Or watch the Mickey Mouse version, *Disney's A Christmas Carol*? Or the Matthew McConaughey movie, *Ghosts of Girlfriends Past*? All right, all right, all right then. Let's revisit the past, think about it logically in the present, and plan for future relationships and how they are connected to the most important relationship of all—your relationship with yourself. I like making lists. I always have, and even more so now because my ex told me they were a waste of time. Once we separated, I started making lists again. So, make a list of all the wondrous, glorious, delicious things about your past life with your future ex.

For example . . .

1. He cooked dinner for me.

2. He knew great wine.

3. He was selfless.

4. He knew great restaurants.

5. My family liked him.

Maybe you have a list of ten or even twenty things that you miss about him. That's only natural. And in fact, it is a beautiful and healthy thing to be able to understand and accept that your ex had a number of positive qualities. Unhealthy, though, is our human nature to romanticize the past. It's tunnel vision focused on the positive feelings and obscuring the reasons the relationship ended.

So, go back and take a look at the first list. Rip out or print out the page and put it on the table right next to you while you make another list: a more honest list. A realistic, unglossed, and not at all romanticized list, expanding upon the allegedly wondrous, glorious, and delicious qualities.

For example . . .

1. He cooked dinner for me . . . but I had to clean up for hours after the meal.

2. He knew great wine . . . which is why he drank a bottle a night.

3. He was good to himself in the relationship and I was secondary.

4. He knew great restaurants but wouldn't try any new ones because they were "just too loud."

5. He liked making fun of my family.

Welcome back to reality.

Moving forward is a scary proposition, hence our desire to harken back to the good old days. But just maybe the good old days weren't all that good. The moral of just about every fairy tale, fable, and formulaic rom-com ever made is that it's never too late to change your future. So, time to make just one more list:

1. What makes you truly, genuinely happy?

2. Who is your support group (your best friends)?

3. What are the qualities you want from a future partner?

A good majority of things we reminisce about in a past relationship never really existed outside of our romantic dreams. Or perhaps they did at the beginning, but by the time the relationship ended, we were dreaming of a relationship that didn't really exist.

CHAPTER FOUR

Falling for Yourself: Inside and Out

*"To keep the body in good health is
a duty . . . otherwise we shall not be able
to keep our mind strong and clear."*

—BUDDHA

Sounds like the last thing a book like this should talk about, but eating right, staying healthy, and exercising are all important to getting back out there as the best version of yourself. Love yourself first, and then allow someone in, to love you. Simply put: balance of mind, body, and spirit. It can be easy to let yourself go when you are upset. Excessive weight gain or loss is not healthy no matter how you split the pie.

After I got married, I did what a lot of us do when we get comfortable: I put on weight. I got sloppy about what I was putting in my mouth both in terms of quality and quantity. Looking back, it seemed like every night my husband and I would eat takeout pizza, or pasta, or chips and queso . . . and sit in front of the television watching reruns of *Friends* or *Two and a Half Men*. Meanwhile, when I looked in the mirror I had what's called a mild form of body dysmorphic disorder, where you believe that your appearance is unusually defective. In my case, I felt like I'd grown to the size of two and a half women. Yikes. It wasn't true, of course, but the fact that my tummy was about to become a muffin top in my favorite jeans was disheartening. I felt fat, and it drove me bonkers.

After my divorce, I realized that I could not let my eating continue the way it had when I was "comfortably" married (my disordered eating then was definitely not a sign of comfort and confidence, but a reaction to a problem I did not want to deal with). I have a friend named Ryan who once told me about his failed relationship with his now ex-wife. When they first met, she was a beauty pageant competitor, so you can imagine the body type. Tall, curvy, and toned! When she got "comfortable" in the marriage, he says, she put on weight. That's when the marriage was at its best. When it started to fall apart, she got back into shape. Interestingly, the relationship had a reverse effect on him. When he was most comfortable, he was in shape. When they started to fall out of love, he put on weight. There's a solid chance you have dealt with one or the other when it comes to your relationship status and your body. I have.

In life after divorce, I had been accused of maintaining a refrigerator comparable to that of a hotshot, young stud lawyer in his late twenties. Ketchup, coconut spread, a tub of grated Parmesan cheese (who has time to grate?), and an unopened bottle of Limoncello that someone gave me as a gift, probably circa 2012. And let me tell you, living life without food and starving yourself is every bit as unhealthy as stuffing your stomach with copious amounts of processed and highly refined carbs, including sugars and starches. This leads to a coma-like state that I have come to know as "Carb Fog." While I often crave just these foods, when I eat them, more often than not, they physically sicken me.

These are important points because, many times, when you

go back to cooking for one, you start to eat badly because you do what is easy and depend on processed, packaged, and prepared foods full of the worst of the worst carbs. Few of us in a bad or traumatic place seriously wants to "cook for one" so "cooking" is more like opening a can, calling the local Chinese restaurant, or, worst of all, drinking your dinner with a chaser of Cheese Nips. Whether you are overeating or undereating, the sad fact is it is cheaper and easier to be unhealthy.

A study by the Harvard School of Public Health and Harvard Medical School found that it costs, on average, about $550 more per year to eat a healthy diet of fruits, vegetables, and proteins. That's $1.50 more per day to eat the good stuff, rather than the cheap, factory-processed, high sugar and starch "foods" filled with twenty-letter-long, multisyllabic additives and preservatives. Sorry about the price difference. We'll talk about financial frugality in other chapters but, to me, the kitchen is NOT the place to make cutbacks. I should also mention that the $550 per year difference doesn't account for the money-saving long-term health benefits. In other words, it costs a lot of money in the long run to eat a poor diet. Good food, as much as anything, is a determining factor in who we are going to be tomorrow and years down the road. The right, good food slows down the aging process and fights disease. Plus, when you eat well, you look and feel better. You'll have more energy, sleep better, and have a more positive attitude. Promise.

The New Single Staples

I know most of you do not want to cook yourself a meal every night from scratch—or even if you do, you rarely have time to pull out all the pots, pans, cutting boards, and knives every night of the week. You don't have to—and you can still be healthy with some strategic shopping. Here's a quick list of food to have on hand that makes creating a healthful meal fast and easy—and delish. Throw them together and you have a salad with a healthy protein that will literally take five minutes.

- Triple-washed bags of salad (my favorite green is arugula)

- Ready-to-eat veggies: organic grape tomatoes, shredded or baby organic carrots, snap and snow peas, celery, and red, orange, yellow, and green pepper

- Veggies that cook quickly with steam or sautéing in olive or coconut oil: asparagus spears, broccoli, summer squash, green beans, triple-washed kale, collard greens, and spinach

- Vacuum-packed or frozen beans: kidney, lentil, black, or garbanzo

- Shredded soy cheese

- Dried fruit (in moderation; the sugar content is magnified in the drying process): cranberries, raisins, apricots, and apples

- Nuts: walnuts, cashews, pistachios, almonds, macadamia nuts, and hazelnuts

- Vinegars: apple cider vinegar (especially those with the "mother" on board), red or white wine vinegar, and balsamic vinegar (in moderation—balsamic vinegars contain more sugar than other vinegars)

- Freshly squeezed lemon and lime juice

- Olive and coconut oils

- Tuna packed in olive oil (limit to once or twice a week because of mercury concerns). I am a vegetarian— but if you eat fish this will work.

- Hard-boiled free-range eggs

 SINGLE FAB FEMALE

Mediterranean Lentils With Rice

This is a Fadal family recipe and I am thrilled to share it with you!

6 cups water

1 cup dry lentils (make sure they are thoroughly washed)

½ cup long grain brown rice

2 diced onions

⅓ cup olive oil

1 pinch Himalayan sea salt

ground pepper

DIRECTIONS:

Sauté the chopped onions in a medium-sized saucepan in olive oil until they are very brown but not burned

Put the rice in a wire strainer and run water over it—clean off the outer coating of starch for about 2 minutes

Once the onions are browned, add the lentils and stir them for approximately 2 minutes to absorb the oil and flavors

Add 1½ cups of water and continue stirring for 1 minute

Add the remaining water along with the salt and pepper

Stir; cover, and simmer for 25 minutes or until the lentils are halfway cooked

Add the rice, stir; cover and cook for an additional 30 minutes over medium heat until rice and lentils are tender.

Add water if the mixture is too thick, but it should be fine once all the water is absorbed.

A-TEAM FEATURE   *The Small Change Diet*

I look for people who know how to inspire and encourage and really live their message. Keri Gans, MS, RDN, CDN, is a nutritionist who does just that.

She's the author of *The Small Change Diet,* and I went to her with some questions about how diet plays an impact and how to help yourself during this time.

DIVORCE OR A BREAKUP IS DEFINITELY A STRESSOR. DIET AND FOOD CHOICES CAN IMPACT HEALTH. WHY DO WOMEN SO OFTEN DAMAGE THEIR DIET WHEN A STRESSOR HITS?

Interestingly enough I have seen women go in both directions when a divorce or breakup occurs—meaning overeating or undereating. Those who tend to overeat are usually looking for comfort in food and it's no surprise that they turn to the food they love; for example, ice cream or anything chocolate. Some go the salty route where chips and french fries become their best friend. At the time of the indulgence a typical women totally forgets what is upsetting her and simply enjoys the taste of the food. Unfortunately, though, within minutes of finishing they usually feel worse off than they did before. Those who undereat during stressful times become so fatigued from lack of food, which provides energy, that they, too, start to feel worse. So, in either scenario, it's not a happy ending.

HOW DOES A WOMAN REFRAME HER ATTITUDE TOWARD FOOD WHEN SHE IS GOING THROUGH SUCH A DIFFICULT TIME?

I always encourage my patients to take control of their food choices, especially during a difficult time in their lives. When everything in your life seems out of control, it can really help to keep your food in check. Healthy eating makes a person feel good and there is no reason to sabotage it. Making healthy food choices can be empowering, and that is just what a woman needs to feel when a divorce or breakup is occurring.

WHAT SORTS OF FOODS SHOULD A WOMAN FOCUS ON THAT REDUCE STRESS AND AMP UP HER ENERGY?

First off, I encourage three well-balanced meals per day and an afternoon snack. It is important that meals (and snack) provide high-fiber carbohydrates (whole grains, fruits, and veggies) for energy, lean protein (beans, fish, skinless poultry) and healthy fats (avocado, almonds, olive oil) to help keep you full for longer. Building meals with fruits and vegetables in general can provide lots of healthy nutrients without lots of calories. Staying clear of fried, fatty foods is recommended, since they can cause you to feel sluggish.

ARE THERE SOME EXERCISES THAT ARE BETTER THAN OTHERS FOR QUICKLY REDUCING STRESS—AND ARE GOOD FOR YOUR BUTT?

I have always been an advocate for choosing any exercise that you will actually do. I find yoga extremely stress reducing, but I have patients who don't. No matter what you choose, as long as you are doing something it is better than nothing. Being sedentary is a stressor unto itself.

LESSONS FROM SMART WOMEN

"A fresh start is scary only because of the power of the unknown, but it's also exhilarating to know that you can help shape your future with the right attitude."
    —Hilary Claggett, Senior Editor, Business, Economics & Finance, ABC-CLIO | Greenwood | Praeger

Party Survival

Before we get to the New Single's diet tips, I do have to make one more confession. I am a cheater. I cheat. I don't cheat often. But sometimes I can't help myself. I don't cheat in relationships, mind you. And I certainly will never cheat on the next person with whom I fall in love. But I do cheat on my diet, from time to time. In other words, it is okay to treat yourself, but not stuff yourself. The temptation to cheat, sometimes, just gets too strong—especially in my line of business where social functions are, for me, *work*. And at social functions, there is food, often rich, decadent, fattening carbo-licious food. Here's how to avoid falling off the wagon at every wedding, bar mitzvah, opening night, book launch, bon voyage, and birthday party where you might find yourself:

1. Nurse your drink

It is very difficult to "nurse" a glass of seltzer and lime or a white wine spritzer for more than about ten minutes. And then you're on to the next and the next and well . . . you know. I don't care how many times people have said it; nursing white wine *doesn't work*. However, it *is* actually possible to nurse something like Scotch on the rocks for an entire two-hour evening, and stay sober, especially if you nibble on crudités. Or, how about a very mild gin and tonic with lime? Or even just a plain tonic water and lime—gin and vodka are mild flavors when set against the astringency of tonic water so you can really fool yourself (and everyone else) into thinking you're having a cocktail when you are simply enjoying tonic and lime on the rocks. Tonic water does have sugar and calories, but compared to several glasses of wine, or a couple of rum and Cokes, it is minimal. If the bar has diet tonic water (they probably won't), that's even better. But I recommend you keep this one type of diet soda on hand at home. Develop a taste for it if you want to control the calories (and carbs) you get from sugary cocktails, liquor, and wine in general.

2. Remind yourself that the food is bad

After attending more catered affairs than I can count, I know that most of the food at large functions is not that good. Most caterers find it challenging to make huge quantities of really delicious tasting food. So before you grab those stuffed mushrooms know they are stuffed with greasy bread crumbs and "baked" in a bath of not very good oil. The shrimp wrapped in bacon is going to be both overcooked and flaccid. If the guacamole is green after an hour you know is has some nasty preservatives in it.

3. Stay mostly raw

Most parties have crudités, fruit, and a decent cheese plate. That's where you want to head. The veggies satisfy your urge to crunch, the fruit fills your craving for something sweet, and a bit of good cheese (two or three half-inch cubes, about three ounces) gives you enough fat to sustain you for the evening, which stops you from indulging in cream puffs. A couple of baby lamb chops serves as satiating protein. But if any of this food doesn't taste really good, don't eat it!

4. Skip the crackers and nuts

I love nuts, but there is no such thing as portion control at a party. One handful of salted peanuts turns into ten. Moreover, that's exactly the kind of nut mainly served at functions—and peanuts are actually legumes filled with carbs. If there are almonds, sure, have a few (ten tops). Keep in mind that nuts are far too easy to eat mindlessly to think counting them out in the palm of your hand at a party is realistic. Ditto for crackers, chips, and bread products. You can't have just one, so don't have any.

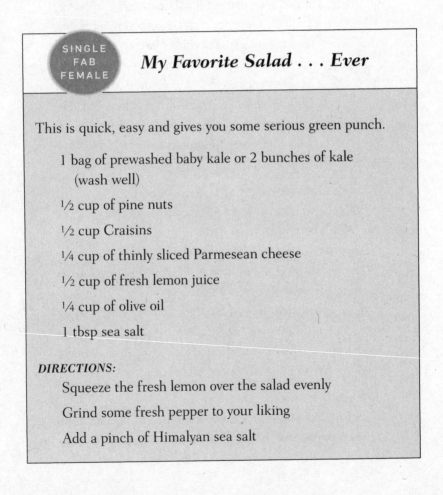

SINGLE FAB FEMALE

My Favorite Salad . . . Ever

This is quick, easy and gives you some serious green punch.

1 bag of prewashed baby kale or 2 bunches of kale (wash well)

½ cup of pine nuts

½ cup Craisins

¼ cup of thinly sliced Parmesean cheese

½ cup of fresh lemon juice

¼ cup of olive oil

1 tbsp sea salt

DIRECTIONS:

Squeeze the fresh lemon over the salad evenly

Grind some fresh pepper to your liking

Add a pinch of Himalyan sea salt

Drizzle olive oil over the top and mix thoroughly

Enjoy! You can have half today and half tomorrow (if you are going to save for tomorrow, don't premix the lemon and olive oil dressing)

5. Leave if you are bored!

This is the number-one way to keep from eating too much at a party. If you are bored at a party, your anxiety level goes up because you naturally feel, "It's a party and I should be having a great time." Anxiety often leads to eating or drinking too much—you eat to fill the hole created by your boredom and unease. I give you permission to leave any party that is dull or no fun. Go for a walk, go to a movie or a bookstore, *anything.* Just get out of there!

Go Whole or Go Home

One of the keys to taking your body back is to eat whole foods. That is to say, foods in as close to their original, minimally processed form as possible. Even the delicious-looking prepared food at gourmet food shops is suspect because you really don't know how it was prepared—with how many processed oils, and with what sorts of breading or add-ons. Certainly ban frozen dinners (even the so-called "healthy" versions) from your freezer. If it is from a box or a packet, I am a serious label reader. And when it comes to produce, I don't mess around. Organics are essential in most cases.

Why go organic? Because some of the best foods for you, when purchased in the nonorganic variety, are likely to hold on to some pretty high concentrations of pesticides, especially those with a thin skin. I mean, you wouldn't season your dinner with bug spray, right? If you are a red meat eater, choose organic grass-fed beef that's growth-hormone free. As for butter, buy unsalted pasture or grass-fed versions because they actually have more nutrients in them than commercial butters and they taste better, too. Margarines are filled with unhealthy fats—the fat in butter is better for you. Grocery stores have gotten wise to consumer demand, and now you can find affordable, high-quality grass-fed beef and butter in most major supermarket chains. Fish should be wild caught for the most part. Chicken should be free range, and that goes for eggs, too. Cheese in its raw form, if you can find it (and you can more frequently), tastes better and in small quantities is very satisfying for our natural and healthy need for dietary fat.

Before you start any new way of eating, you should consult your physician. My friend Karen turned her health and her mood around by changing the way she eats—and started burning fat as fuel. She even got off medicine to treat her type 2 diabetes, a chronic condition often brought on by eating the wrong foods and gaining weight. "I gave up all the 'fattening' carbs, such as bread, pasta, baked goods like my morning muffin, and so-called low fat diet products—which I discovered often contain unhealthy trans fats. I focused exclusively on leafy and cruciferous greens (spinach, broccoli), eggs, grass-fed animal proteins, nuts, and all kinds of fresh berries." The result? "I lost fifty pounds, and felt more energetic and clear-headed, and far less depressed. I was able to get off my post-breakup Prozac." Once Karen looked and felt better, it seemed almost effortless to reenter the dating scene, which she did with enthusiasm—and success. "I'm in a happy relationship with a guy who shares my passion for healthy eating. He's helped me become much more active, and I have the energy to keep up with him on hikes and biking trips," she says.

LESSONS FROM SMART WOMEN

"With the right 'team' of support, anyone can come through the very difficult divorce process a more self-aware, happier person."

—Karen Bigman, founder of the Divorcierge

THE BIG O: ORGANIC MUST-HAVE LIST

Here is the Environmental Working Group's list of twenty-six kinds of produce you should buy in organic form, as they have a tendency to hold the most pesticides, even after washing for a minute under fresh running cold water:

Apples	Cherry Tomatoes	Cherries
Strawberries	Snap Peas	Pears
Grapes	Potatoes	Tangerines
Celery	Hot Peppers	Carrots
Peaches	Blueberries	Green Beans
Spinach	Lettuce (Green	Winter Squash
Sweet Bell	Leaf, Romaine,	Summer
Peppers	or Butter)	Squash
Nectarines	Kale	Raspberries
Cucumbers	Plums	Broccoli

The New Single's Power Produce

Here are my top organic fruits and veggies, and the benefits they bring to your body:

AVOCADOS   Yes, avocados are fruit. And yes, they are incredibly good for you. In fact, this is as close to a perfect food as you can get. Why do you think all of the fabulous people in California have avocado on everything? Each avocado contains four grams of protein. Plus, they're good for your brain.

BLACKBERRIES   Loaded with antioxidants and vitamin C. Plus, the seeds are little miracle workers, containing omega-3 and omega-6 fatty acids.

BLUEBERRIES   They don't call it a superfood for nothing. Blueberries are loaded with vitamins, nutrients, and fiber. And, they're known for fighting cancer.

GUAVAS   Buy guavas now. One guava is like eating four oranges, when you're talking about vitamin C. Plus, they're high in dietary fiber.

STRAWBERRIES   Another one of the superfoods, strawberries are cancer-fighting and heart-protecting powerhouses.

KALE   Satirist John DeVore says, "Kale is iceberg lettuce that won't shut up about what it read in *The New Yorker*." That's hilarious, but kale's not as snooty as it used to be. However, it's definitely smarter than iceberg lettuce. It's loaded with antioxidants, vitamins, and minerals. Kale is a proven aid in preventing breast and ovarian cancer. And, fun fact: it's one of the fastest-growing baby names in America. Two hundred sixty-two Kales were born in 2013. Ever think you'd name your child after a vegetable? Yeah, that's how good Kale is.

SPINACH   Cancer-fighting, bone-building, blood pressure–reducing, and totally versatile. Eat it raw, sauté it, or juice it. You could easily eat spinach with every meal.

SWISS CHARD   Unlike the cheese of the same nationality, there are no holes in what Swiss chard has to offer. It contains a whole alphabet's worth of vitamins, plus fiber and antioxidants.

The New Single Goes Nuts . . . and More

You have to admit, there's something cool about knowing what's so good about good food. But if you really want to get serious about a life-changing diet for your New Single lifestyle and beyond, then here is how we go a step further. Drumroll, please . . . nuts and seeds! What? Doesn't sound exciting? Or is it that you're too afraid of feeling like a hipster? I have the following list of nuts on hand at all times. I put a small handful or about a quarter cup of each nut in small resealable snack bags to maintain portion control—which I've already mentioned is often difficult to keep track of with nuts. Aside from the health benefits, they give me energy and let me know I'm giving my body a little extra loving.

Almonds

Walnuts

Cashews

Chia seeds

Flaxseeds

Hemp seeds

Macadamia

And then there's the **goji berry.** They're not actually nuts or seeds, but that's probably where you'll find them in the health store. Dried goji berries are an excellent antioxidant, and can also be found in powdered form for the shakes at the back of the book. Finally, I have a few more favorites:

CUCKOO FOR COCONUTS　　Coconut oil helps you burn
more fat. Populations that eat a lot of coconuts are
among the healthiest people in the world (they also
aren't eating a lot of processed carbs, sugars, and
starches). I use coconut oil on practically everything.
From my food to my hair and skin—it's like the
Dexatrim of natural food. As for slathering my body in
coconut oil, it's great protection against hair damage, it
improves dry skin, and it's a natural sunscreen. Why
do you think suntan lotion smells like coconut oil?

OLIVE OIL　　When I am not using coconut oil, I'm
probably putting olive oil on everything else. Olive oil
is a big part of the Mediterranean diet. It was what

I grew up on. Basically, people from that part of the world have longer life expectancies and lower risks of heart disease, high blood pressure, and stroke. The average Greek citizen consumes about six and one-third gallons of olive oil per year, but the Greeks have a longer life expectancy and a lower rate of heart disease than people from other European countries and North America. Scientists don't know for sure if it's the olive oil (Mediterranean people who are eating a traditional diet do not eat many processed foods and certainly not many refined carbs), but it doesn't hurt. If you're feeling like a sad sack about your lost romance, one study by a university in Spain found that olive oil appears to protect against depression. It's happiness in a bottle.

SINGLE FAB FEMALE

Tips for Juicing

I love juicing. I love combining amazing natural flavors and feeling how much energy my body has afterward. Here are a few of the combinations I love when it comes to having a quick pick-me-up.

Kiss Me Kale Juice

3 large kale leaves (I always remove the thick part of the center)

3 stalks celery

1 apple

1 inch peeled ginger root

juice of 1 lemon

Green Girl Power

2 stalks celery

1 Granny Smith apple

¾ cup parsley

juice of 1 lemon

½ cucumber

Melon Makeover

1 cup cantaloupe

1 cup watermelon

3 stalks kale

6 strawberries

2 tablespoons cashew butter

SINGLE
FAB
FEMALE

Tips to Stay on Track

- Keep a small bag of nuts or almonds on hand. They are quick to prepare and easy to eat. The protein will keep you feeling full, and you won't have to eat a lot of them to feel that way.

- Avoid carb-heavy meals. They may make you feel comfort, but as soon as your blood sugar spikes and then plummets, you will feel hungry again.

- Drink a lot of water. There are all sorts of flavor-infused waters these days that won't add sugar to your diet, but will taste great. Keep hydrated to keep healthy.

- Eat when you are hungry. Don't wait until you are starving. And don't skip meals because you are upset, too busy, or trying to lose weight.

- Avoid sugar. I know for a fact that sugar affects my mood. I avoid eating sugar as often as possible. This is not a time for mood swings.

- Too much caffeine is not good and can make you irritable. I was a caffeine junkie for a long, long time. I still love my coffee, but I have since tried to drink as much decaf tea as possible. I love David's Tea shops, which have a huge variety of fun flavors to try and don't make me miss so many cups of daily caffeine.

Snacks on the Run

Never let yourself get hungry—that's a recipe for "I'll just have this doughnut or cookie." Carry smart snacks with you—here are some portable suggestions, easy to pack into a reusable, lidded container:

WANT TO EAT	DECIDE TO EAT INSTEAD
2-pack Reeses Peanut Butter Cups	Single organic dark chocolate peanut butter cup
Kettle Chips	Alive & Radiant Quite Cheezy kale chips
Granola bar	GoMacro Cashew Caramel Protein Paradise MacroBar
Chips and salsa	Beanito chips and lentil dip

TOP 8 ANTIAGING FOODS THAT HELP HEAL

I know that a food section seems like the last thing an advice book would have, but how you eat and what you eat affect every single aspect of your life and your feelings about yourself, your body, and most of all, your confidence. I have included a list of foods that are good for antiaging, but are also helpful in keeping you happier, more alert, and healthier.

green tea	sweet potatoes
seaweed	avocados
walnuts	berries
pumpkin	garlic

A-TEAM FEATURE   *You Are What You Eat*

There are some foods that fight stress. Toby Amidor, MS, RD, national nutrition expert and author of *The Greek Yogurt Kitchen: More Than 130 Delicious, Healthy Recipes for Every Meal of the Day* (Grand Central Publishing, 2014), talked with me about what foods help stabilize your mood, especially during a time like this.

WHAT FOODS ARE BEST TO STAY AWAY FROM DURING A STRESSFUL TIME LIKE A BREAKUP OR DIVORCE?

During stressful times, many people tend to dive right into their high-calorie, high-carbohydrate comfort foods like macaroni and cheese, fried chicken, french fries, cookies, cakes, and ice cream. I would recommend staying away from those foods until you regain control of your emotions and are able to mindfully control portions. For example, instead of eating the entire quart of ice cream, enjoying a half-cup of vanilla ice cream topped with fresh fruit and a spoonful of crushed peanuts.

WHAT FOODS CAN HELP THE MOOD DURING A TIME LIKE THIS?

These five foods can help alleviate some of the stress experiences during a breakup or divorce. Eating these in conjunction with exercising can help alleviate the stress even more.

WHOLE WHEAT PRETZELS   Many people turn to carb-rich foods and there is a reason why! After eating foods high in carbs, the brain releases a feel-good chemical called serotonin. If you're going to eat carbs, then make sure they are whole grain. The USDA's Dietary Guidelines for Americans recommends making half your grains whole. This way you are alleviating stress and eating healthier all in one bite.

NUTS   During a divorce or breakup, your stress levels are high and can last awhile. High levels of stress can run you down, leaving you open for sickness. Nuts like almonds, pistachios, and walnuts are high in vitamin E and zinc. Both of these antioxidants help boost your immune system, plus they are good sources of B vitamins, which also help your body cope with stress. Nuts are high in healthy fat, so to keep calories in check, keep portions to a small handful or a quarter cup.

YOGURT   During times of high stress your stomach may be acting a little wonky (bellyaches, diarrhea). Probiotics found in Greek and traditional yogurt can help calm your digestive system and keep it in tiptop shape. You will also get a nice boost of protein and calcium with every spoonful.

DARK CHOCOLATE   Research shows that dark chocolate may help lower levels of stress hormones. Chocolate also contains sugar (a type of carbohydrate), so it will also stimulate the release of serotonin (a mood-improving hormone). This doesn't give you the green light to indulge in chocolate all day long. Chocolate still has sugar and a boatload of calories. Enjoy a one-ounce portion of dark chocolate once a day MAX—that should do the trick!

SALMON AND TUNA   Fatty fish like salmon and tuna help manage adrenaline levels to help keep you calm and collected. Omega-3 fats are also good for healthy skin and hair—which will help boost your self-confidence and make you more gorgeous for your next romantic interest.

SOME NEW SINGLES DON'T REALIZE HOW THEY EAT IS JUST AS IMPORTANT AS WHAT THEY EAT. WHAT DO THEY NEED TO REALIZE ABOUT FOOD TYPES?

Eating mindfully helps decrease overall stress, which can help keep calories at bay, especially if you're a stress eater. Eating mindfully involves an awareness of the foods you eat, the environment you eat in, and your hunger cues. Many people don't pay attention to unhealthy habits, which can lead to weight gain such as mindlessly munching on chips in front of the television or eating on the run. When eating mindfully, you want to utilize all your senses: tasting the food by enjoying every bite, eating in a quiet environment or with pleasant conversations, smelling the aromas, and looking at the variety of colors on your plate.

Here are five ways you can eat mindfully.

MAKE TIME TO EAT   Don't try to eat while on the run or while driving. It just makes for a stressful environment. Instead, set aside ten to fifteen minutes so you focus on enjoying your food.

ASSESS YOUR HUNGER   Oftentimes people confuse stress and hunger. Think about how hungry you really are before heading to the kitchen to grab a bite.

SAVOR EVERY BITE   During stress eating, people shove food in their mouths and don't really pay attention to what they are eating or how the food tastes. Instead, slow yourself down by taking a bite of your meal or snack, closing your eyes, and focusing on the flavors while you slowly chew your food.

CREATE A PEACEFUL ENVIRONMENT   E-mails, phone calls, and even the news can increase stress. Turn off all electronic devices. Invite friends or family to enjoy a meal together and enjoy the art of good conversation.

SELECT TASTY FOOD   There is a misconception that healthy food cannot be delicious and that is far from the truth! Healthy, delicious recipes are a click away on the Internet or can be found in many books, including my new cookbook, *The Greek Yogurt Kitchen: More Than 130 Delicious, Healthy Recipes for Every Meal of the Day.*

CHAPTER FIVE

Unclutter Your Life, Declutter Your Heart

"I was once afraid of people saying,
'Who does she think she is?' Now
I have the courage to stand and say,
'This is who I am.'"

—OPRAH WINFREY

When I started writing this book, my goal was to answer the questions I have been asked since my divorce: How are you doing? How did you get through it? Did you do the right thing? Did you really try to work it out? Best advice you ever got? What did you learn? The list goes on.

In that barrage of queries, though, no one ever asked me the most important question: How did you take care of yourself through your breakup? The truth is, no matter if you have no children, six kids, two dogs, a cat, or parents to take care of, if you do not take care of yourself first and be selfish for a little while, NO ONE will get taken care of. Yes, we can all be SUPER-WOMEN, but we cannot do it operating from a deficit. I didn't believe this for a long time. Now my motto is: Focus on yourself. Only then can you focus on everyone else. You need to be whole before you can give anything. Without a whole you—you will always only be partially there. You will continue down the path of patterns that have not served you and will not serve anyone around you.

Learn to Love the Sound of "I"

Sounds easy enough, right? Focus on yourself. The truth is, for me, it was extremely difficult. Having to spend time with my own thoughts? Having to spent time facing the truth? I was a forty-something divorcée with no children, renting an apartment, saddled with my postdivorce debt and a very public divorce. The hardest thing for me to do at that moment was to be honest with myself about who I was . . . I was frustrated that I was starting over again and that I was alone. So, I had to take life one minute, one hour, and one day at a time to be able to get real with myself.

I spent a lot of time writing and focusing on living in the present. I was determined to be happy with who I was today in order to thrive tomorrow. It is never easy to quiet our thoughts and listen to what we are supposed to do next or who we are going to be, but take ten minutes a day to try and do this. In a short amount of time, you will find a large number of answers that come from within.

Sexy Self-Talk

I am a big believer in the fact that everything starts from within, even, maybe especially, physical beauty. Despite the fact that I built my career in front of the camera, I truly believe that if you don't have internal peace and happiness and come from a good place, your inner discontent will always come to the surface. Remember the letter my friend wrote me? For a long time I heard myself joking around about my ex. Trying to make light of the situation, trying to be the tough girl who wasn't affected by this and would get through anything. I did it with my family, my friends, and with the people I work with. I saved the "real me"—the sad me—for just one friend and for my pillow.

My self-talk in the months following my divorce was extremely negative. "I knew marriage was a bad idea." "I will never get married again." "I grew and he didn't." Yes, I said it all. I used my external self to convince my internal self of how I felt. I spent some time traveling the world. I was in France, Italy, Dubai, Canada, all over the US, and back to Italy. Travel helped me wake up to see who I really was, the person I had forgotten about while trying to make my relationship work. In between trips, I started to see the therapist that my ex and I used to see together. It was then I was able to hear my words aloud. And boy, were they scary.

Over time, I realized that my self-talk was self-destructive. It was filled with excuses and denial, both ways to protect myself from the truth. I remember leaving the therapist's office one Friday morning and deciding as I walked up Sixth Avenue in the West Village that something had to change or I would be making this same trip forever with no different results. At that moment, I decided to take control of my negative self-talk by composing a list of the things I should be saying (needless to say, I did not need a list of the negative stuff).

Here is my original list, with some additions from along the way:

- Protect yourself.

- Today is the future.

- You are living your life.

- You can't have other people make you complete.

- You can't fix people.

- You can only fix you.

- Decide what you want.

- Go after it. 100 percent.

- Stop seeking advice from everyone.

- Don't settle. Ever.

- Stop confiding in everyone.

- Keep a journal, diary, Post-it. I don't care what it is. Just keep track of yourself.

- Go outside often.

- Take a walk with a friend.

- Force yourself to go out alone.

- Force yourself to go out with someone.

- Remember that before you love yourself, you must like yourself. It is essential, just like it is when it comes to finding a relationship.

LESSONS FROM SMART WOMEN

"After witnessing divorce in my primarily female population of patients for twenty-two years, and then going through my own divorce two years ago, I learned a few lessons.

1. Take charge of the divorce. Sometimes lawyers can make things take forever, and this costs you more. Find a good mediator, put your children's best interests at the heart of the divorce, don't use them as the pawns, do your best to only say nice things about your soon-to-be-ex-spouse. Divorce is about two adults who don't agree, the children are innocent bystanders, keep their hearts safe and out of the line of fire. A mediator will help smooth things over and get things done for less money.

2. Find a therapist who specializes in blended families and divorce for yourself and the kids. Look for someone to give you good parenting skills. This is not the time to let boundaries go by the wayside because you feel guilty. The kids need the structure and love, now more than ever.

3. Take care of yourself. Keep your eating and exercise routines in place as much as possible. You have to take care of YOU, or you won't be able to take care of anyone else. Become a morning person. Get up early and exercise, even fifteen to twenty minutes a day is better than zero. Get your day and food planned first thing . . . make your bed . . . you'll feel as if you have accomplished something first thing in the morning.

4. Maintain a relationship with a therapist for a couple of years! It takes that long after your divorce to really get a handle on what life looks and feels like. It's a grieving process and takes time."
—Dr. Kristina Sargent, chiropractic physician and founder of Restor Healing Center

Date Night

This date night is all about you. You don't have to get a manicure, pedicure, or a wax for this date night. Perhaps you will do those things on this date night, because it is all about what you want to do with yourself, for yourself, or about yourself. To this day, I dedicate one night solely to me. While it was a night that I originally dreaded, it is now a night I look forward to immensely. It is a night about *me*.

You will learn that this night is essential to your self-care and self-love. It helps you figure out who you really are and who you want to become. It doesn't have to be at night, by the way. It can be a Saturday morning or a Sunday afternoon. The only requirement is that it needs to be time that is all about you.

Here is what my Saturdays look like—religiously, without fail, as long as I am not traveling. If I am, I simply change the day. I get up and head right to Starbucks and I treat myself to my favorite drink, an Iced Americano. Then, I pack up my yoga mat and go to my favorite yoga class. This is the one sacred time in my week that my phone is off. Totally off. For someone like me, that is not an easy feat, but it is one that allows my mind to wander and my heart to remember what I am truly passionate about.

After ninety minutes in yoga I head to my favorite juice bar and continue my day with thirty-two ounces of kale lemonade. You might think this is an acquired taste, but I love it. Next stop, the A train to the West Village.

The West Village was a place I avoided for a long time following my breakup. It held too many memories of young love, and it was difficult for me to wander through the streets alone seeing one couple after another strolling around and holding hands. In time, I stopped focusing on those couples, and you will, too. If I do see them, I don't see them with disdain, now I simply smile and say "one day," if it's meant to be. While I am downtown, I go in and out of shops, I check out a new restaurant or I have lunch at a sidewalk café. I spend time with me. At the end of the afternoon, I put myself back on the radar. I am refreshed. Renewed. And rewarded by the fact this builds my self-confidence. Take care of yourself. Make sure you do and do it often. It will be the best gift anyone can ever give you.

Here a few ideas for your date night or date day, as mine is called:

- Practice yoga with a teacher and a class that makes you feel comfortable.

- Take a new class for something you are interested in learning about at a local community college or adult education center—Renaissance art, creative writing, kayaking . . . whatever.

- Buy a new book and read it at a sidewalk café.

- Go to a movie you would never usually see.

- Walk around the park and photograph nature.

- Find a new place or neighborhood to explore in your city or region.

- Treat yourself to a spa service you have never had.

- Get a massage.

- Take a bike ride.

- Go for a drive and stop someplace new for lunch.

In Chapter 3, we talked about setting long-term (one-year, five-year) goals. Now I want to talk about some short-term measures to carry you through the next three months of your life as a New Single. This is one of the most important things you can do—because it helps keep you looking forward. I found that I needed to set some very simple goals for myself when it came to self-care. I started with the self-talk on the inside, but of course the outside is also important. Let's take my self-care goals one by one, and see how they could work for you, too.

Goal 1: Pamper Your Body

Yes. Undress more. Obviously, within reason and in the right environment. But to me, it is critical for you to fall back in love with yourself. However you decide to do it. I put two huge full-length mirrors in my newly decorated apartment. I walk by them all the time. I used to not look at myself. I had not seen my body and self for a long time. Both literally and figuratively. Now, (blinds shut) I feel proud to be fully exposed. I no longer hide from myself. We often take care of anyone and everyone else in order to avoid ourselves. I have to indulge and give my body what it needs. I take care of it, inside and out. From frequent massages to emptying out my bathroom and replacing almost all of my bath products with healthy alternatives. I feel in love with a line called Shea Moisture. (You can always find it at Target.) It's natural and it makes me smile every time I use it. Again, these things sound simple and perhaps even silly, but when I walk out of my house, I do it proudly and with purpose, and all of these things contribute to the confidence I continue to work on every single day.

A-TEAM FEATURE *Skin Sense*

Stress can take a toll on our bodies and especially our skin—there is no question about it. Dr. Shirley Madhere, a New York City holistic plastic surgeon and owner of Jet Set Beauty Rx, shared some advice on how to take care of yourself both inside and out.

WHAT IS IMPORTANT FOR YOUR SKIN, ESPECIALLY FOLLOWING A STRESSFUL TIME?

During periods of stress, your body will undergo chemical and hormonal changes that will lead to increased inflammation. Inflammation is thought to be a factor in a number of medical conditions as well as premature aging. So, if you want to stay healthy as well as look good for your age, keep this process under control by employing these top holistic methods for healing and total body wellness: be mindful of the anatomy of the experience, acknowledge your emotional pain, and allow yourself the process of healing (without prolonged or excessive lament or regret); believe what is meant for you will be for you, and have faith that all will work out as it should for your highest and best good; examine what you learned from the experience and use that to make the best of your present moment and future.

- Eat well (nutritiously)—at least three cups of greens and low glycemic fruits daily

- Stay well hydrated by drinking ample (unsweetened, nonalcoholic) liquids

- Get adequate exercise, specifically cardio

- Manage stress with techniques for a sound mind such as meditation, yoga, breathing techniques, tai chi, massage, etc.

- Avoid picking at, overstripping, and overstimulating skin with devices or harsh products

- Keep a healthy skin regimen with cleanser and skin-appropriate products

- Keep skin moisturized

Is caffeine bad for me?

Interestingly, there are studies to argue the benefits as well as the negative effects of caffeine—in limited doses. Nevertheless, too much caffeine may be both dehydrating and overstimulating (with a "crash" later). In addition, if you are adding sweetener, the sugar has detrimental effects on your skin and your waistline.

WHAT IS A GOOD FACIAL CARE REGIME TO FOLLOW?

The best facial regimen for you will depend upon your skin type, current condition, lifestyle, and commitment to healthy, beautiful skin. In general, a simple protocol involves three steps: cleanse (without stripping), treat (any skin issues), and moisturize (adding sunscreen).

ARE THERE ANY FOODS I SHOULD EAT AND/OR AVOID?

It has been shown that a whole-food, nonprocessed diet with minimal sugars and starches has maximal benefits on wellness and longevity. So, while a specific nutritional program is best based on your blood type or unique DNA (which may make you more sensitive to carbs than other people), adequate daily intake of the following will help to keep your skin looking radiant: a) green, leafy vegetables, b) vitamins A, B, C, D, and E and multiple antioxidants from fresh, whole fruit and organic animal foods, c) water, and d) protein from natural or organic sources. Regardless of type, avoid excess sugar, starch, fried foods, processed "foods," GMOs, and char-grilled foods.

HOW OFTEN DO I NEED FACIALS, MICRODERMABRASION, OR TREATMENTS?

Whether you would benefit from additional cosmetic options such as facials and microdermabrasion or aesthetic medical procedures, for example, injectables or plastic surgery, depends upon a number of factors related to how you are aging:

- How you manage stress

- Your diet

- Your skin hygiene

- Whether you exercise

- What you inherited (genetics)

- Your personal beauty philosophy

- Your budget

- Time: if you are willing to commit to maintaining healthy, radiant skin

- Your current skin condition

- Your mental attitude (negativity is expressed in facial lines)

Goal 2: Give Your Body What It Needs—Movement!

Working out has always been an important part of my life. I have changed it up over the years from running to weights and then cross training. But, after my breakup I realized that exercise was important to me mentally as well. I started devoting myself to yoga. Up until then, I had been a huge naysayer when it came to yoga. I used to think—if I don't sweat, what's the point? Well, I could not have been proved more wrong.

Yoga allowed me to take that time I needed for myself. To

unplug, without apology and to focus on the poses and on my mantra each class. To this day, I am a yoga devotee. I am in a class at least three or four times a week—daily if I can swing it. It is something I never dread (like I used to dread running) and it is meaningful on a number of levels.

When you love yourself, you allow yourself to stay in tune with what your body is asking of you. My body wanted me to spend time with it, and to love it and allow it to heal in a number of different ways. Whatever your form of exercise—devote yourself to it. Carve out the time, no matter how busy you are. This is a time where you need to come first.

Following a breakup or divorce you can feel exhausted physically due to the fact you are mentally drained. But physical activity releases endorphins, which will make you feel good both inside and out. Exercise reduces the amount of stress hormones that are released by your body. During this time, facing so much stress, there is no way to argue that finding a park, a gym, or a good exercise trainer or program is key to taking care of yourself.

A-TEAM FEATURE   *Go Yogi*

I love yoga. And I do a lot of it. But I wanted to talk to an expert about the benefits of it and the fact that if you have just twenty minutes a day, you can reap some of the benefits. I consulted New York City yoga instructor Michael McArdle.

What are the benefits of yoga—especially for someone who has just gone through a breakup or divorce?

I embarked on my first yoga training without the slightest suspicion that this discipline would grow to become an integral part of my daily life. The beauty of it directly relates to the benefits because it forces you to reconnect to both your mind and body. That is something that is especially important and beneficial for the recently divorced or newly single. Very often the aftermath of those scenarios will make the person going through it feeling isolated and alone. Yoga demands you surrender to your breathing, you become more fluid and very aware of your inner self while becoming more awakened to your surroundings. Beginners often feel intimidated walking into a yoga class for the first time. Taking a few private classes can allow you the confidence and knowledge to feel comfortable in a group setting, which is key after surviving a breakup or divorce. Yoga also helps alleviate all forms of discomfort and directly aids in healing. Let's just say, yoga and divorce are a "perfect marriage."

Will yoga give me a good workout—what if I don't sweat?

I started yoga about fifteen years ago—I got tired of weight training, my schedule didn't allow me to play sports as much, so I'd lost a lot of cardio and muscle training and thought I'd never find a "good workout" again. I was thinking about yoga and thought it was low results and very spiritual, and I was like, "can I sit through this?!" But as it became more popular, it became more dynamic, and suddenly I was getting the best workouts of my life by doing it. The best part is, you can't "burn out" on yoga, so it's sustainable through the decades! Not sweating during it isn't a deal breaker, but truthfully, if you are surrendering to the form you'll experience a sweat.

IS THERE A FAST YOGA WORKOUT I CAN DO?

Yoga is something you can do at home, and I think you can get in a decent flow in about twenty minutes. Even if you can't take an hour and a half to go to a class, a short yoga DVD or video will help stretch everything that you need to stretch, let you get in some strength conditioning, and best of all reconnect you to your breathing. It's not a time-consuming task if you build up knowledge of what works best for you. A good teacher will help you in that area.

Goal 3: Head to Toe

Sounds silly, right? Hair and nails? What business do they have in a post breakup/divorce guide to finding yourself again? Turns out, they have a lot to do with it. Nurturing and pampering yourself is key, even when you have no time, no money, or no interest. Pedicures, manicures, haircuts, hair color, and blowouts were real relaxation for me. For one, during a time when I didn't feel attractive inside or out, they gave me a little boost in self-confidence. If you don't have the funds to go to your favorite salon, use a coupon site and find deals that will often give you 40 to 50 percent off services to bring you in. Or, find a local beauty school in the area. I go to one in Midtown that specializes in facials costing a fraction of what most spa facials cost, and the students work extra hard to get everything just right.

Goal 4: Aromatherapy

Scents played a large part of making over my home (and me). I love the smell of coconut. It reminds me of summers in Florida when I was younger and used to hang out in college and spent time by the pool or at the beach. I purchased a coconut and vanilla candle for each room in my apartment and, after work, I would light them and just melt into my newly created life. It became something to really look forward to, and I still do each day. In fact, as I am writing this, two of those candles are burning the midnight coconut oil with me.

Your favorite scent might be lavender, patchouli, or lemon. If you have never experimented with how fragrances alter the ambiance of your home, give it a try. Scented candles and scent diffusers are inexpensive and widely available at stores such as Home Goods or TJ Maxx. Give them a try.

Goal 5: Dress

My "look" as a New Single has definitely evolved. I am less concerned about how I look for other people and much clearer about how I want to look for myself. Of course, all of this is built from the inside, but it transforms your outside appearance as well. Work on your wardrobe. Get rid of the dress you wore when you both first went on a cruise together. Lose the jewelry (sell it!) he surprised you with one night. Make sure the only things in your closet are items that hold the memories you are building to move forward as the New Single. This is your time.

This is a foundation you are building for the future. Make sure it is strong.

Goal 6: Sleep

I had quite the love affair with the predawn hours when I moved to New York City to work on the early news. I was up every morning at 2:30 A.M. I took in the views of the Chrysler Building and 57th Street seemingly alone for a long time. I had no choice but to be up early, but I also had an immense desire to live life to its fullest by burning the candles at both ends. Sleep was overrated, I thought. In fact, I only got about four hours of sleep a night and I seemed just fine. Truth is, I probably wasn't. Between working on the air and working on saving my marriage, those hours dwindled even more over time.

Eventually, I came to realize that it was critical to find the time to sleep in order to reenergize myself for my life. As I moved into my life as the New Single, I was determined to start taking care of myself—no matter how many hours it took out of the day. I am certainly not perfect, but I am always working toward a goal of at least seven to eight hours of sleep a night to make sure I am alert, making clear decisions, and looking my best.

Goal 7: Vitamins

My cousin Shannon is a health guru. She is vegan. She is gluten free. She reads every single label at the supermarket. And, she knows her vitamins. Not long after my breakup she came to New York City and stayed with me. During that time, she redid my kitchen from top to bottom, including my vitamins and supplements. Thanks to Shannon, I have a daily vitamin regime. From coenzyme Q_{10} to iron to B vitamins that helped me during the more stressful times, I am faithful to my supplements and vitamins. I start each day with a Mediterranean protein shake by PureTrim made of all-natural ingredients. It gives me tons of energy.

I also make my own shakes and I have learned about juicing, especially green or veggie juicing. After my divorce, I felt it was crucial if I was starting over to start over all around. I realized that eating right, concentrating on whole, unprocessed, or minimally processed foods gave me energy to deal with life's stresses. I don't turn to french fries (though I eat them from time to time) when I am upset. I deal with the problem at hand in a methodical way. Eating right and taking vitamins as part of my daily regime is a lifestyle—not a diet or a temporary part of my life. It is like breathing. I just do it naturally because I know it's right for me.

Goal 8: Therapy

I didn't grow up in a family where therapy was something you did. In fact, I had never even heard of it until I was twenty-six years old. I was in television and I was sure that I needed to be skinny to be successful. I was anything but skinny. I was athletic and I ate carbs. But, to the camera and to my head, I was fat. I was counting calories, burning them off with ridiculous amounts of exercise and purging. It wasn't until I dropped down to 103 pounds (I'm five foot three and one-half) that I realized losing weight was a problem instead of an accomplishment. It was becoming an obsession. It was not until my father found me unable to walk down a flight of stairs that I would admit there was a problem. Therapy helped me before my eating disorder became unmanageable.

So, therapy was the first thing I turned to when I knew that I was about to go through another big change in my life. Don't get me wrong—my friends were fabulous, but sometime friends don't give us the advice they want to give us for fear the truth could hurt a friendship long term. A good therapist can be a guide and a supporter to whom you can pour out your heart without worrying about jeopardizing a friendship. If you have a good therapist, I suggest weekly visits until you feel you can take them down to twice a month. If you don't, be very diligent in how you select one.

I recommend finding someone who specializes in family and relationships so that your therapy will be specific to what you are dealing with. Shop around. Make sure you are comfortable with the person you have chosen. And make sure you are honest with her or him. If you are not prepared to tell the therapist the truth (the whole truth, and nothing but the truth) don't waste your time or your money sitting in her office for an hour once a week. You won't get the help you need, and you will leave the therapist's office feeling worse than when you entered. Make sure you make the most of it and give yourself the gift of an amazing new start.

Goal 9: Home Is Where the Heart Is and Where It Heals

I have always been a minimalist. Clutter has never been a friend of mine. In order to sit down and write the desk has to be clean. In order to enjoy my dinner the kitchen can't be a mess. When I leave for vacation, the house is clean despite the fact that no one is going to be home. So, it came as a shock to me that my heart was very cluttered following my separation and eventually my divorce. I was not sure who I was, where I was going, or what to do next.

My home suddenly became very important to me both as a refuge and as a symbol of my new beginning. Either way, I was determined to start over again and declutter the things that were mentally and emotionally blocking me.

I realized that after my marriage ended, I was avoiding my home. I was doing anything that I could to stay away from it. I didn't feel good being there. I would spend an entire Saturday roaming around the city—in and out of the same stores—to make sure I didn't have time by myself in my home. One Sunday morning, I woke up and realized my home was not the problem, how I was treating it and treating myself was the problem. I didn't leave the house that day. I decided to declutter EVERY-THING.

A writer friend of mine called me around the time I was re-arranging my home. When I told her what I was doing she said, "Tamsen, you can't paint away the memories of your marriage." Maybe not (see pages 121–125 for tips on redoing your digs and the benefits it brings). But I *could* put a fresh coat of self-love into my life and that is exactly what I did.

I chose to remain in my marital apartment, so I knew that I had to replace the items that caused me to see memories of my past versus visions of my future. From the size and color of my couches to my bedding to my lingerie, I used my "alone time" to rebuild who I was and who I wanted to be moving forward.

The Boudoir

I started with the bedroom since that was really the most important place for me to begin. As I mentioned earlier, I traded in my king-size bed for a queen. First, it didn't feel as empty. But more important, I remembered I never really wanted a king-size bed to begin with. I am all of five foot three and one-half and he wasn't that much taller. I thought a queen was comfortable and would keep us close. We ended up with a king. It was what my husband wanted. He liked to spread out in bed and have a lot of room. I knew when we were standing in Macy's that the bed was way too big for a Manhattan apartment. It was huge. It took up the entire bedroom. The day it went out the door, I could not have been happier. It was dark brown. I opted for a white bed with white sheets and white bedding. New. Fresh. A beginning. I painted my bedroom walls a slate gray, bold but simple. It was me. I added a big painting of a flower above my bed to remind myself every night I was just starting to bloom and grow all over again. Perhaps you don't need to be as symbolic, but for me it continues to work each day.

These Walls Should Talk

From the bedroom, I quickly moved to the public rooms of my apartment. In their current state, these rooms were packed with items my ex and I had purchased together, or received jointly as gifts. They represented "us"—not "me" though, so as lovely and thoughtful as they were, they had to go.

Understand that this was not easy. One gift, a wedding gift, was particularly difficult to deal with. It was an incredible art installation on the wall of our living room given to us by an artist friend. My original thought was to keep it so as not to insult my friend. In retrospect, I should have taken it down the moment we separated, because every single time I looked at it I felt a mild wave of nausea sweep over me. The art no longer spoke to who I was and the emotions I was now feeling. It had to go. In its place I put up a picture of a red poppy sitting delicately in a wheat field. I am sure it was taken in Italy, the country I love to visit as much as I can. The image reminds me of the power that I have as a single woman. I never get tired of looking at it. It makes me smile. I believe it gives me power.

You don't have to spend a fortune to make these changes. I went to Home Goods, Overstock, and to sales all over the city to find what I wanted for a new beginning. It took determination and patience. So, if you don't want to put a strain on your plastic, take the time to find what defines you and hang it up. Then, embrace that power. You are on an adventure to embrace, not trapped in a life you are trying to escape.

Some recent divorcees try too hard, in my opinion, to escape their past. I am thinking of a story a friend once told me about a friend of hers, Rory, who'd gone on a smash and burn spree after her ex left. One evening Rory invited her girlfriends over for gossip, wine, and fine china destruction. That's right. Rory asked her friends to join her in tossing the Haviland dinner service her ex-in-laws had given her as a wedding gift out the window—literally. The result: thousands of dollars of gorgeous plates, cups, and saucers on the ground, in smithereens. What a waste. Worse, this little act of vandalism didn't make Rory feel one bit better, and it definitely left a bad taste in my friend's mouth.

Get rid of whatever marital "stuff" is weighing you down—but do it in a grown-up way. Acting like a vengeful child feels like, well, a vengeful child. And you are a woman.

Paint Your Heart Open

I am not artistic. Creatively, I don't have that gene. My dad is an architect. My brother and sister-in-law renovated their entire house themselves. It's amazing. Me, on the other hand? I can't even hang a picture let alone paint one. But that didn't stop me from enlisting the help of some friends to help me paint my heart out. New walls give your place a new look and feel. I now have a red kitchen. Yes, it's called poppy red. And it makes me smile every time I flip the light on. I have a slate gray closet, a chalkboard column in the corner of my living room, and Tiffany blue furniture that I painted on a rainy Sunday just for fun. That painted furniture went from "about to be on Craigslist" to my most treasured possession.

Closets

I left my ex's closet empty for a long time. In New York City, that's saying something. Heck, I could have rented that space out for a profit to storage-deprived Manhattanites. I had a tough time accepting that I was alone again and kept the space empty "just in case." When I did finally really embrace my fabulous singlehood, I took over that closet space with gusto. In no time, I had four amazing color-coordinated closets in perfect order. They give me a solid and organized foundation to begin each day. There's no where-is-that-pink-blouse chaos to contend with before I've had my coffee.

I have to have a lot of clothes for work, so it is essential to keep myself organized. For me, organization is the key to happiness. So, let's help you get organized in your New Single life. I have a few tips from personal organizer Andrew Mellen, author

of the book *Unstuff Your Life*. From my desk to my closet to my
e-mail—Andrew has been essential in helping me to understand
that uncluttering your life is not an option; you have no choice
because otherwise you cannot unclutter your heart.

A-TEAM FEATURE   *Unstuff Your Life*

I am always meeting exciting people in my line of work and
Andrew Mellen is definitely one of them. He is an expert on
the subject of uncluttering things you no longer need and author of *Unstuff Your Life*. What better person to talk to about
letting go of all the things that weigh your down and keep you
from moving on?

HOW DOES CLUTTER IN THE HOME AFFECT CLUTTER IN YOUR HEAD OR "EMOTIONAL CLUTTER"?

Physical clutter is often a concrete representation of mental or
emotional clutter as well. An inability to stay focused, regardless
of the cause, typically results in piles and stacks and clumps of
items set down randomly throughout the home and workplace.
Clutter is a series of deferred decisions. When we're overwhelmed,
distracted, or distressed it's easy to set an object down and keep
walking. You may have the best of intentions of later collecting
that item and returning it to its home, or you may have been so
preoccupied that setting it down was completely unconscious.
They both yield the same result: clutter.

　　Living with clutter and disorganization exacerbates an already stressful situation. When you can't feel safe in your own home, you're repeatedly stressing your adrenal system. That level of stimulation makes it that much harder to concentrate for long periods of time. Add in the almost constant interruptions available through digital media and electronic devices, and you can see why many people collapse in a heap of frustration and exhaustion over something as simple as not being able to find their keys, wallet, or bag.

Ensuring that your home is organized and functioning smoothly reduces stress and lays a foundation for greater peace and serenity. From that foundation you have a much better chance of navigating the emotional upheavals that accompany the dissolution of any intimate relationship.

WHAT IS THE BEST WAY TO GET STARTED WITH DECLUTTERING?

The best and easiest way to get started decluttering is to get familiar with The Organizational Triangle®: One Home For Everything, Like With Like, and Something In, Something Out. One Home For Everything means one home and only one home. It doesn't matter where that home is, just that there is a home. So where you keep your keys may be completely different from where I keep my keys, but your keys have a home. They're only one of two places—in your hand unlocking something or in their home. Apply this principle and you'll be able to find anything in thirty seconds or less.

Like With Like means all like objects live together, not most or some. That means all your office supplies live together, all your cooking utensils live together, all your important papers live together. This ensures that when you go to the home for something you'll find everything you're looking for at one time. These two principles together will solve 85 percent of all organizational challenges.

The last leg of the triangle, Something In, Something Out, is all about achieving stuff equilibrium. That means you have enough of everything that serves you and nothing that doesn't. There are no rules about what "enough" looks like—your space will do an excellent job of communicating that to you. If you have piles and stacks of papers or other items lying around your home and they don't have a home, then you have too much stuff. If your clothes are bursting out of your closet and you claim you never have anything to wear, you have too much stuff.

Chances are on some level you can sense when you're trying to fit more into a space than it can comfortably hold. Letting go of your willful insistence and yielding to the space's limitations is the first step. Determining what enough looks like for you establishes your baseline for this principle. Once you've determined what enough looks like, you're no longer in the business of accumulating—regardless of how cheap, expensive, or unusual the item is. You're now in the business of replacing, not augmenting. Applying this principle is all you need to do to stay organized for the rest of your life.

How important is it to ask a friend for help?

Never underestimate how helpful friends can be when it comes to getting and staying organized. Friends are an invaluable asset, whether they are serving as a "clutter buddy" and actually helping you in your organizational process or just keeping you company while you do your own tasking. The simple act of relying on a friend as an external source of accountability will increase your success geometrically.

WHAT DECLUTTERING GOALS SHOULD WE BE SETTING?

It's easier to describe how to set goals rather than defining what the goals should be. It's always helpful to pick the area or category of stuff that upsets you the most as the best place to begin. That way you get a great return for your initial efforts.

Set goals for yourself that are specific, realistic, and reasonable and that also require consistent efforts. Never attempt something as vague as "cleaning out the garage"—there's no easy way to quantify how long that would take. The better way to state that goal would be to say, "I'm going to spend three hours cleaning out the garage," and then setting a timer for three hours and getting to work. Now we have an achievable goal: working for three hours in the garage.

Regardless of how much you get done, when the timer goes off you've accomplished your goal. The more specific your goals and consistent your outcomes, the stronger and more confident you become. The timer becomes your ally in quantifying all tasks that are impossible to quantify otherwise. Never work for less than fifteen minutes or more than three hours at a time. Less than fifteen minutes is not enough time to get much done on projects the size of a garage or even a closet. And after three hours your ability to concentrate will fade. That's the time to take a break and check your e-mail, get a snack or walk the dog—anything to break your concentration and refresh yourself. After a break, you can set the timer for subsequent three-hour blocks of time, just be sure to take a break between each one.

Be sure to take "before" pictures—these are crucial for those moments when you think you're not making enough progress fast enough. A story might kick up that says this is impossible and you'll never make the kind of change you want to make.

First off, don't pay attention to any story that includes "never" or "always." They are seldom true. And given that the goal is not to complete something other than working until the timer goes off, the photographs will show you that you are making progress, even if isn't your progress doesn't look like what you imagined. Implicit in the goal is change, and the photographs illustrate that regardless of how you feel, change has occurred. That should be enough to counteract any story to the contrary.

Don't fall into the trap of thinking that you don't need a break after three hours. You might be quite exceptional in any number of ways, but when it comes to stuff, there are no exceptions. Stuff is inanimate and will outlast you every time. Failure breeds failure and success breeds success—set yourself up for success by relying on the timer.

WHAT KINDS OF ITEMS SHOULD A DIVORCED WOMAN CONSIDER LETTING GO?

Certainly putting away anything that causes you grief, shame, or regret is a great place to start. Given that you are probably extremely vulnerable and emotional, I'd suggest starting with the easiest choices first. Things you were holding on to only out of a sense of obligation can be the first to go. If any of those items have significant value, you may consider selling or auctioning them off and investing the funds in some thing or some experience that clearly represents who you want to be postdivorce.

Next I'd suggest turning your attention to those things that are isolated to just you and your former spouse. Leave things that involve children or extended family for a bit later. Consider whether you can use this item in your new life or if it will always remind you, and not in a pleasant way, of your relationship. If the item in question has use and no upsetting associations, integrate it among your other belongings. If it will always upset you when you look at it or use it, let it go.

For those things that are just too tender to interact with right now, I suggest you box them up and put them someplace safe to return to in six months. Label them carefully including the date you placed them in storage then schedule an appointment with yourself six months from now to revisit the project.

Remember, it's only stuff. You bring the story to all of it—in and of itself, each item is neutral. We each endow every object around us with meaning. You can tell yourself a different story about any particular item if you want to. It's helpful to examine your motives if you seem to keep telling yourself upsetting stories when no one's listening. Not that you're to blame, but you do have the power to change a story at any time.

WHAT ARE THE BEST WAYS TO MAINTAIN YOUR NEWLY UNCLUTTERED SPACE?

The Organizational Triangle® is all you need to stay organized. Applying the first two principles will get your home organized and applying the third principle will keep it that way. Once you've achieved stuff equilibrium, ask yourself the following questions before you bring anything home:

- Do I really need this? Why?

- Do I already have one like it?

- Is it better than the one I already have or do I just like it more?

- Where will it live?

- What will I do with it?

- When will I use it?

Answer the above questions with specific answers. "Just because" is never a good enough answer. And even then I suggest you take a picture of it and defer buying it for thirty days. You'll be amazed how little makes it home from a store after considering a purchase for thirty days. Consider how you spend your time—you may imagine yourself lying in a hammock reading magazines but if that's unlikely, consider how many subscriptions you really need to periodicals you never get around to looking at.

It all comes down to your core values—what matters to you and how aligned your actions and words are with those values. The world is full of beautiful and practical things—it's also full of useless trash. Curating your home and your life to accurately reflect what is important to you is essential to staying organized. When you become more focused on experiences and living your values, you discover you don't need much to physically make that happen. That's the best place to be.

My Secret

Victoria had a secret for a reason: she knew that what a girl wore underneath could make or break her day. Your lingerie or undergarments are helping to build your foundation, no pun intended. Yes, it sounds corny. Believe me, when I was tossing perfectly good lingerie into the Salvation Army box I thought I was crazy. But, I have come to realize that I had no choice. If you are wearing something that conjures up memories of days gone by, it has to go. Replace it one piece at a time. You need this change to embrace your inner beauty and surround yourself only with what makes you feel good.

I am a Hanky Panky girl. They are pretty. They are lace. And even if I am the only one seeing them—they make me smile.

 A-TEAM FEATURE

Got Style? You Better Get Some!

So, how do you get back out in the dating world and, more important, in style, so that you feel amazing and not awkward or uncomfortable? I turned to celebrity stylist Amy Acton, who has helped me with my on-air wardrobe, to find out about closet staples for the New Single.

HOW SHOULD WOMEN GO ABOUT REINVENTING THEMSELVES THROUGH THEIR WARDROBE?

Remember your age! I am a firm believer that at a certain age less is more. Women are at their most attractive from their midthirties all through their forties and into their fifties. Therefore capitalize on this. Don't muddle up the best-looking years of your life by hiding behind a mask of makeup or by overstyling your look. Believe me, you are beautiful! Let that inner God-given beauty shine through and do most of the work for you.

Let's face it, by this point we know what we like and what works for us. Sophistication is SO sexy!!!!!

As women, when we go through a breakup we tend to make drastic style moves . . . RESIST! Don't chop off your hair, get a tattoo and, if you have never worn black leather, do not rush out and buy the tightest leather skirt you can find! Trust me, you will not be able to pull it off with the confidence necessary. That is not saying it isn't time for a change, just be smart about it.

If you feel you want to try some "younger," more "current" trends, introduce them subtly and slowly. If you are itching for leather then by all means go for it! However, try some pants, a pencil skirt, or leggings with a little leather trim or embellishment. Cut your hair but opt for a different style without a major length change and if you love it go a little shorter each time. Please resist getting a tattoo altogether, but if you must, get it somewhere discreet.

Think about who and where you are and who and where you expect to be over the course of the next few years, and plan your makeover accordingly. The old rule: dress for the life you want, not the one you have holds so true at this point in time. Most important, you cannot allow yourself to fall into the depression staples of yoga pants and T-shirts. It is paramount that you feel as good about yourself as possible so make the effort. If you look good, you will feel even better!

It is a good idea to call a professional for help and believe me, it is an expense well worth it. Hiring a good personal stylist will definitely save you not only time but money in the long run. They will create a makeover plan that works for you and your new lifestyle. They will give you the objective and honest feedback on what works and does not work for you, your lifestyle, and your body type that your friends and family are not capable of. They will also prevent you from spending money on items that aren't really going to do you justice and will end up just taking up space and collecting dust in your closet.

WHAT IS MOST IMPORTANT ABOUT YOUR FIRST POSTDIVORCE DATE OUTFIT?

The most important thing about your first postdivorce outfit is that you feel and look confident, beautiful, and empowered!

WHAT DO CERTAIN COLORS SAY ABOUT US?

It is said color is a very powerful tool. I use it in my work every day. In a postdivorce makeover situation it is important to utilize colors that lift your spirits, make you feel good, and exude that as well. Reds, pinks, yellows, greens, and blues should be your go-to colors.

> RED: is said to evoke the feelings of joy, love, and sexuality.
>
> YELLOW: is said to evoke freshness and joy as well as intellect.
>
> BLUE: is said to evoke feelings of knowledge, power, and trustworthiness.
>
> GREEN: is said to evoke feelings of harmony, peace, and calmness.

I suggest using gray and black as anchor pieces. They should almost always be offset by some color. Gray is said to evoke feelings of lack of commitment and black is taken as morbid and too serious.

That being said, purple should be avoided at this point in time. It is said to evoke feelings of nostalgia, sadness, and gloom.

WHAT ARE FIVE STAPLES EVERY WOMAN SHOULD HAVE IN HER WARDROBE AS SHE STARTS OUT ON THIS NEW JOURNEY?

The perfect-fitting blue jeans and simple white tee. This is a classic that looks good on every woman at every age!

The LBD. No woman should be without the perfect little black dress. Throw a jacket or sweater over it for the office and sans, you can wear it to almost any social event as well.

A statement piece of jewelry. This doesn't have to be expensive, it just needs to make a statement. Maybe a funky cuff bracelet, some chandelier earrings, or a cool necklace.

A simple layering piece. Perhaps a great blazer or a simple cardigan. Something that will work well over the jeans and tee and the LBD.

And most important!!! At least one pair of ridiculously expensive kick-ass heels that you can wear all day and then dance the night away in. Trust me NOTHING makes a women feel more empowered and ready to take on the world than a kick-butt pair of shoes! I promise it will change your life . . . or at least your outlook on it.

Goal 10: Be a List Girl

I love making lists. I always have. But when it came to falling for myself and figuring out who I was again and how to get back in touch with life, I lived by a list. If you are not a list-maker, you may want to give it a try. I have spoken to many women who say that they lose track of the days and are not able to stay focused. They spend time looking at old e-mails or fretting about what their ex is doing instead of looking forward and working on their own lives. If this sounds familiar to you, then you really need to take up making lists. Use your lists to guide and encourage your progress through your day. Your lists will keep you from looking back over your shoulder at what was.

Goal 11: Live for Someday Starting Today

I am a creature of habit. If I like something I stick with it. I was not a sports girl so I don't play tennis or golf or volleyball. However, I am a curious person. I love to learn and have found that this is a great time to learn something new. Why? Because right now everything is okay. The world is yours. Embrace it. I used to coach a woman who moved from New Jersey to California. She loved the water and in time decided that after her husband died she didn't want to deal with the winters anymore. After a lot of planning and a lot of bad matches online, she decided nothing was holding her back from moving across country. She works for herself in the entertainment industry, so she was able to make the transition. Being on the West Coast was actually an advantage.

We would check in from time to time and I would follow her updates in the way we all do now—social media. Then I was sitting at work one night and she texted me, "Call now!" I was a little worried because we had not spoken in a while, so I immediately picked up the phone. She answered by the second ring. "Guess what? I have taken up rowing. I am in my first long ride tomorrow and I couldn't be more excited about it. Wanted to share and see what you are up to. I have been getting up every morning at six o'clock to row, tomorrow is a big day."

I had never heard of her doing much besides an occasional visit to the gym around January of each year, so I was somewhat surprised. I said, "Why rowing?" She answered, "Why not? I decided I'm not sitting at home waiting to do things. I am afraid someday won't come—so my someday is today." With that, I added an eighth day to my week: SOMEDAY. And, I embrace SOMEDAY like it's today. I no longer wait to do things. I do them now, because now is about us and it's about time.

Things to try for SOMEDAY—*TODAY*:

- Rowing

- Pilates

- Dancing

- Half marathon–running

- Pottery

- Painting

- Computer classes—the Apple Store has some great ones

- Social media classes

- Museum membership

- Golf, tennis, or any other sport you desire

A-TEAM FEATURE   *Your New Space*

Cathy Hobbs, ASID/LEED AP, is a nationally known interior designer and the owner of Cathy Hobbs Design Recipes, an interior design and home staging firm based in New York City. She's also a dear friend of mine whom I go to whenever I have a decorating dilemma. And I had one after my divorce. I didn't move but I wanted my apartment to look different than it had when I was married. Oh, did I mention that Cathy is also a five-time Emmy award winner, nationally syndicated columnist, and was a finalist on season six of HGTV's hit reality show *Design Star*? She is! Visit her at cathyhobbs.com. Here are her tips for making your place feel new—and very *you*.

Begin with the Bedroom

In refreshing one's home I view it in the same way I would suggest one reinvent one's life. Start from the inside out. The first place to begin your home reinvention is in the nest, your bedroom. Your bedroom should surround you with a sense of serenity, privacy, and calm. That bed you purchased together, bedding, all need to go. Purchase that gorgeous, feminine bed you have always wanted. Then, focus on truly wrapping yourself in sensual softness. I call it "dressing the bed." Here is my design recipe for making it the perfect boudoir.

- Purchase a good quality mattress. You *will* want a new one, trust me.

- Add a feather bed on top. There is nothing like sleeping on down!

- Purchase thick cotton sateen sheets. I prefer pure white with a basic border pattern or pretty decorative piping.

- Dress the "top of bed" with the bedding of your choice. I say the more toss pillows the better. Think fun, funky patterns to contrast with your duvet set and don't be afraid to toss in some beaded pillows or ones that are furry or with a tassel or two!

- Add wall sconces on dimmers or purchase those that use candles. Soothing, calm lighting will rest your mind at the end of the day.

- Layer a scent. Soy-based candles and scents such as lavender (place fresh lavender in tiny cheesecloth pouches and place them throughout the bedroom) can open your senses and refresh your mind!

Kitchen

The kitchen is truly the heart of the home and no doubt it will be filled with items from your wedding registry, no matter how long it has been. For many, kitchen items don't hold the same sentimental value as, let's say, the wedding dress. If you can use it, keep it. No need to replace all of those pricey gadgets you already own. Still want to refresh? Purchase a kick-butt coffee-maker. I mean it, splurge, there is nothing to get you perky in the morning like a good cup of joe! Buy or make yourself a "me" mug, a quirky cup perhaps in your favorite color to give yourself a quick "pick-me-up" each morning.

Living Spaces

From the family room to the living room and other spaces throughout your home, the reminders are endless. Perhaps you have a family room where you and your ex enjoyed movies with your children on family night, or your dining room reminds you of the many occasions you and your ex entertained family and friends at your gracious dinner table. Renewing, refreshing, and reinvigorating these spaces can go a long way to recharging your life and giving you a fresh outlook.

First, think color. Go ahead and paint that accent wall you always wanted or add that soothing or bold graphic wallpaper print that reflects your personality.

When it comes to redoing your space, pay attention to the large items first and then focus on the smaller details.

Here's my design recipe for creating the ideal living space:

- Purchase or select an inspirational piece you love from your existing furnishings and build a palette around it.

- Purchase any big-ticket items first. Select pieces that are high quality and nontrendy so that they stand the test of time.

- Accessorize. The right accessories and artwork are like the icing on a cake. I love art, so why not purchase a piece of art, perhaps from a graduating art student, to add color and texture at an affordable price.

Color

I am a huge fan of color. When it comes to creating your oasis, the color should reflect your personality and taste—and it should be upbeat and make you feel happy and alive. When looking to refresh your space, one of the first must-do design "makeovers" I would suggest is to change the color palette. A fresh color palette can serve as the foundation of your décor. Keep in mind that cool colors can create a mood of serenity and calm, while warm colors create feelings of warmth and coziness.

If you're afraid to make a bold statement with color, then why not just paint an accent wall? Stumped about which colors would make great accents? Think warm and inviting or bright and bold. Yellows, oranges, and greens all make great accent colors and can easily blend with lots of color palettes. Stay away from muted or pastel tones as they do not make great colors for an accent wall and are best suited for all-over color. Accent walls should make a bold statement so that they stand out as opposed to blending in.

Design Recipe Color Dos and Don'ts
Dos

1. Do consider using neutrals such as black, charcoal, gray, or beige as the foundation for your color palette then pair it with a bold accent color.

2. Do select a signature bold accent piece and build a color palette around it.

3. Do consider black and white as potential bold color statements.

4. Do consider an accent wall if you're afraid to commit to a strong accent color in the entire room.

5. Do bring color into your décor through accent pieces such as artwork and accessories.

6. Do consider using cool colors in a space that you want to visually enlarge or create a sense of calm and serenity.

Don'ts

1. Don't just tie yourself to one shade of a bold color, consider tints and tones of the same color.

2. Don't be afraid to mix vintage pieces with modern.

3. Don't use colors that are too grayed down or muted.

4. Don't use colors that are too warm in small rooms, it can make a room look smaller.

5. Don't be afraid to "go bold".

6. Don't paint the ceiling a color, it will close in a space.

Manifest Your Future

I first heard of a vision board years ago when I was running the matchmaking business. At the time, my only vision was trying to get through each day and make sure we had all the people matched appropriately. I was working a full-time job and running the business aspect of the company. The idea of adding another task or obligation to my plate was daunting. My favorite vision was that of closing my eyes each night for a few hours of sleep before starting over the next day. Once I went through the toughest time of my divorce and starting rebuilding all areas of my life, I decided to take some time to look into a vision board and what it was really all about.

Bottom line, a vision board is a collage of images and pictures and all the things that make you happy. There are so many ways to do it now. Pinterest is perfect for this. In fact, you can search and find ideas and ways to create your own digital vision board on Pinterest. The good thing about it is that you have a community to share it with if you so desire. It is about dreaming and attracting. I have always believed in the law of attraction so I set out to make my own. In time, I had a theme: Own Your Power. I decided to find positive affirmations, pictures, and any words I could find that helped me do this. In time, I had a pretty incredible dream board. It is one that I continue to add to today. I am able to help other people and, perhaps just as important, empower myself to understand where I was and where I want to be. Every day is a journey.

Goal 12: Schedule Yourself

Yes. Remember the Jim Carrey movie when he said yes to everything. Well, I am not saying to be crazy about it, but I want you to schedule yourself. Keep your lunch dates. Make meetings that will help further your career. Find things to do. Take that extra yoga class. Book another playdate for the kids. Say yes to everything within reason for a little while. Keep a reasonable but full schedule, while also keeping time for yourself packed in there. You will meet people along the way and you will also find that you have less time to worry about being single or looking forward wholeheartedly to that next date or hating your ex. This does not mean to exhaust yourself so that you don't have time to think, but it does allow you to realize there is life outside the one you have been living and it's important to start embracing it. The only way to go forward is to look forward.

A-TEAM FEATURE *Rut Check*

I checked in with Peter Shankman, customer service and marketing futurist and best-selling author of *Zombie Loyalists: Using Great Service to Create Rabid Fans*. He gave me five ways to tell if you are in a rut career-wise and how to break out of it. Check out his daily blogs at shankman.com.

Nothing is more dangerous to professional life. Ruts are

dangerous, because much like illegal drugs or any Aaron Sorkin project, you don't realize you're stuck in one until it's too late, when it's really hard to quit. (Think about it—did you even CONSIDER, for a SECOND, leaving *The West Wing* when we were waiting for President Bartlet to announce if he was going to run again? Of course not.)

Ruts can be business killers, especially when times are good. It's too easy to get complacent when the fire isn't under your butt at 300 degrees.

Ruts also come when you've had a few down months. Even though you're busting your butt, you might feel like you're on a hamster wheel, and there's no end in sight. That's also a rut, and it's also dangerous.

So—First: Five ways to tell if you're in a rut.

THINGS ARE GOING GOOD   and you feel like your company could run on autopilot for a while. There's a reason pilots don't leave the cockpit unattended while the plane is on autopilot. Because something could go wrong. Autopiloting your business is dangerous—you don't get to see the shifting landscape, and you can't react in time when threats emerge. So if you feel like you could just chill for a month or so, you might be in a rut, and it might be time to shake things up.

YOU'RE BORED   Boredom is dangerous when you're running a business. There's no excuse to get bored in the real world, and there's certainly no reason to get bored running a business. If you're bored, it means you're not doing anywhere near enough hustling.

YOU'RE NOT HAVING FUN ANYMORE   Let's face it—we become entrepreneurs because we love working hard, and in the end, it's fun for us. When we're not having fun, that's a huge, huge warning sign. Something is wrong, and needs to be addressed ASAP.

YOU'RE OUT OF IDEAS   This is a dangerous one. Without new ideas, we can't continue to grow. Without growth, there's no innovation, and without any of that, kiss revenue goodbye. Ideas are key. If you're out of ideas, you could be in a rut.

FINALLY, YOU FEEL LIKE YOU'RE SPINNING YOUR WHEELS I'm very familiar with this one—it's the worst feeling in the world. The rest of the world is doing things, and you're sitting there, feeling like you're wasting time. There's nothing worse than that kind of rut.

So . . . What do we do?

How to Break Out of a Rut

By physical definition, a rut occurs when the same thing happens over and over, carving a hole or indentation into an object. While this is awesome when water does it to make the Grand Canyon, doing the same thing over and over again in business is a guarantee to fail.

YOU NEED TO SHAKE IT UP!   Perhaps that's doing something as simple as getting into the office thirty minutes earlier each day and reaching out to long-lost contacts, or perhaps it's having "walking meetings," outside, to get the blood pumping, instead of sitting at a boring table in a boring conference room talking in the same boring voice.

RUTS OCCUR WHEN PEOPLE ARE RESISTANT TO CHANGE You simply can't be afraid of change and expect to succeed. Don't take crazy risks, but take calculated ones. Calculated risks have built our great nation. Be daring. Client says he wants it one way, and you believe it should be done another way? Do it both ways, and present them. I used to do this all the time when I was a photographer. Works wonders! The goal is to try new things, to change, and reap the rewards.

MEET PEOPLE OUTSIDE OF YOUR INDUSTRY, IN THE SAME BOAT YOU ARE I can't recommend Masterminds enough. Essentially, a Mastermind is a collection of eight to ten people, all in different industries, all in a room for a day. You spend a half hour on each person, where that person introduces themselves and explains the challenges and problems he's facing. Then the rest of the room chimes in with their suggestions and issues. Why is this awesome? Well, let's say you're in real estate. You're so head-down in your real estate world that you might not be able to notice other good ideas. But the guy who owns the bakery? He's not in real estate! He might be able to suggest an amazing idea you never would have thought of, because he saw what you're doing from an entirely new perspective. New perspectives are key. You can get them in a Mastermind. Added bonus: I hold Masterminds all over the country. Click on the "contact" page and let me know if you'd like to join in your city!

EXERCISE AND CHANGE WHAT YOU EAT! Look, entrepreneurs are passionate, and we work until our heads explode. That's no secret. But—and this is a big but . . . we need to have balance. I've found that the best way to get that balance is exercise. Whether it's early morning runs, walks, or bike rides, or midday spin classes, yoga, or Pilates, or even an evening weight-lifting session, nothing clears your head and puts you in the right frame of mind better than a workout. It's chemical. Your body releases endorphins. Endorphins are the happy drug. They let you work better, smarter, and with higher quality results. Why do you think I skydive? I do my best writing after jumping! Nothing kills a rut faster than a shot of endorphins from the brain to the body. Nothing.

ADDED BONUS Drop 80 percent of the carbs you eat, and replace them with vegetables. Drop 80 percent of the alcohol you drink, and replace it with water. In other words, try and focus on eating natural food. Veggies, lean meats, etc. Give up dairy if you can, as well as anything processed. Eat real food. Or, as your grandparents called it back in the day, "food."

FINALLY, TRY DOING GOOD ONCE A WEEK FOR OTHERS Whether it's volunteering at an animal shelter (by the way, get a pet if you don't have one, they're amazing at busting you out of your rut), working at a soup kitchen, or even helping out an elderly neighbor, two things happen when you do this (and that's not even including the good you're doing!). First, you see things from a different perspective. You get to understand a segment of society to which you might not be accustomed, and you can learn from them. Second, all the most creative/ successful people volunteer. They understand that in addition to the good they're doing, it's a way to let the universe help them—i.e., giving back allows for new ways of thinking, and new ways of thinking are the building blocks for getting out of a rut.

Goal 13: Lose the Soul Suckers

Have you ever said to yourself: "Everybody sucks." Well, you were partially right. Not everybody, but a lot of people do suck. They suck the happiness, the spirit, and the life right out of you. Or, for something a little less uncouth, let's go back to freshman-year philosophy and Jean-Paul Sartre: "Hell is other people."

There are people in this world that are so unhappy with themselves that they want to bring you down, too. I know; I have been one of them, and I have had more than a few of them in my life over the past few years. They are chronically dissatisfied. When you are happy, they want you to be sad. When you are there with an actual problem, they are there to listen, but they are not there to hear. They listen just long enough so they can complain. They are the soul suckers.

I had a coworker who sucked my soul dry as often as he could. He has always been a soul sucker. For a long time, though, I did not realize it. Conversation after conversation with him, day after day, I would find myself mentally exhausted. I could feel him taking my positive energy and destroying it. Any time I would muster more, he would latch on to that as well. It was a daily appointment with an emotional vampire.

We spoke each day—in fact I enjoyed the company—especially at a time when I thought I needed to be down. But about a year ago, I decided that I needed to be more self-aware. I discovered that my soul was being drained and I, myself, was doing it to other people. I wanted to turn my life and my mood around. When it came to my coworker, however, the emotional draining continued. I could feel unnecessary hatred and anger welling up inside me, once I got in tune with myself. Over time I learned to shield myself from it. In other words, I learned to set boundaries. I would be present in the conversation but only superficially. No more complaints from my end. Polite head nods and smiles. And the negativity went in one ear and out the other. In time, I have learned to do that naturally with people. If you have not set boundaries, it is time.

How do you spot a soul sucker? Or, how do you know if you are one?

1. S/he never asks about you.

2. S/he constantly has an issue or drama she needs you to fix.

3. Nothing but negativity. S/he never sees the positive side of anything.

4. A constant need for affirmation (and it's never enough).

Tell yourself it is okay to close yourself off a little. It's okay to put an arm's length between you and most other people; it doesn't mean you are unkind. It is simply a way to preserve your positive energy source for the times you need it most. This is not to say that we should be anything but courteous and loving to the people around us, but we must always maintain our distance from people who are taking more than their fair share.

Do you remember that quote by Sartre: "Hell is other people"? That's only true if you make it true. Perhaps you want to take advice from his lifelong relationship partner, Simone de Beauvoir, instead: "Change your life today. Don't gamble on the future, act now, without delay." Lose the soul suckers.

CHAPTER SIX

Mr. Right vs. Mr. Right Now—The Next Ninety Days

*"You know you're in love when you can't
fall asleep because reality is finally
better than your dreams."*

—DR. SEUSS

My Father's Toast

On the day of my wedding, my father made the toast. He was beaming with pride. I knew he would be. His little girl—all grown up. As he looked across Tavern on the Green at all of my closest friends and family members, he raised his glass and said, "May this be the day that you loved each other the least." Not a dry eye in the house. Even the *New York Times* reporter was so touched that my father's toast and benediction closed out his article.

As a New Single, I realized that day was the day we loved each other the *most*. When I started to see men after my divorce, I kept my father's toast in the back of my mind. It became a kind of mantra for me, and on more than one occasion helped me understand the difference between a date who was fine for

"Mr. Right Now," but nowhere near the kind of keeper "Mr. Right" would be. In this chapter, we'll talk about men in general— whom we'd like to date in a new relationship, whom we'd like to avoid.

Bottle of Red

Everyone has a type. Until they don't.

When I went back out on the market, for example, I started dating older men. That is what I was convinced I wanted. About a year later, I met a younger man, and all that changed.

I used to believe that I would only date older men. My justi- fication being he would have his life together, both financially and emotionally. An older guy would know what he wanted. Then, one night I went on an accidental date with a younger man. I'd known him for about four months, and the truth is I didn't really like him, much less think of him in terms of attrac- tion. In fact, I didn't really feel anything for him at all. We coexisted in a small world that, somehow, led us to make plans to discuss an entrepreneurial idea. Definitely not a date and defi- nitely strictly business, and we both (thought we) knew it. And how could it be anything but business? Because even before we even hit the front door of the bar, this guy had ripped my idea to shreds. Jerk. Sometimes, however, timing is everything.

We walked into a little wine bar in the East Fifties. This place was different, like some secret world. Exposed brick walls and, in the back corner where we hid away, an old steam pipe wrapped from ceiling to floor in rope. He shook the server's hand as he walked past.

"Hmmm . . ." I thought.

He ordered a bottle of wine without even asking what I liked.

"Can we get a bottle of the Côtes du Rhône? I love this," he said, turning toward me, "and I love Paris."

Interesting thing I've since learned about Côtes du Rhône: it's not showy; it's unassuming. It's not the focus of the conversation; it inspires conversation. At the time, the only thing I remember thinking was: "I thought the Professor was the only one who knew how to order wine." Turns out, allowing myself to have an open mind allowed me to realize there is more than one answer to a problem, and perhaps more than one "type" of guy out there for me.

I think back on that moment of discovery very fondly. I was so adamant that I knew what was good for me—older men—when in reality, at that time in my life, a younger man was just what I needed. I learned that sometimes it really is best to just live in the moment and let the unexpected unfold.

As is the case with wine, so it goes with prospective partners; don't have such a rigid preference or palate that you close yourself off to any possibilities. There are a lot of good men out there—let this next part of your dating life "breathe" and just maybe you will find a surprising new person to open a bottle of vino with as well.

Learn Who You Are Now

Easier said than done, but it is possible. Remember, the dating scene changes all the time. Even if you've only been out of it for five years, it's going to look different when you jump back in. It sure did for me. If you're in your forties, don't run around like you're in your twenties, going out to nightclubs and partying all night. If that was never you to begin with, trying it now may feel awkward. You run the risk of being miserable. Maybe bowling is your thing—so go bowling! Or go to an art exhibit, the theater, whatever—but make sure you're being true to yourself.

Case in point: Julia, a fortysomething woman I know in Los Angeles, was ready to get back into the dating scene about three months after her divorce was final. In her twenties and early thirties, she would hit the trendy Hollywood bars with girl-friends (her "posse," as she called them back then) and they'd tag team—talk to a guy that one of them was interested in and then make the introduction. At forty-six, she knew that wasn't really an option anymore. And going out with a group of women didn't exactly match her level of maturity. She also thought meeting someone her age who matched her level of sophistica-tion in a trendy LA bar was somewhat unrealistic.

Instead, Julia looked at all the things she liked to do, and figured out a way to pursue them in a social setting. As a PR pro who really loves her job and profession, she does a lot of speak-ing but felt she could always hone her skills. So she signed up for a public speaking seminar offered by a professional organiza-tion. It was the sort of event that attracted as many men as it did women (Julia quickly learned that wine tasting and cooking classes attract mainly females) and she did, in fact, meet a couple of guys whom she dated casually. These "trial run" dates were a good way to hone her dating chops, since she was a bit rusty after being married for twelve years.

Julia also started attending more PR conferences and events—not only did it polish her resumé and her skill sets, it put her in contact with many men who were in her age group and were intellectual equals. Simply by being very active in her field, including getting involved in industry-sponsored charity events, Julia met and dated a lot of men. She is still playing the field but she's having a great time. "I feel like I'm meeting many very nice people who are, by default, helping me figure out what I want in a man the second time around."

Your Ideal Man Might Not Be Your "Perfect" Man

We all have a list of the good and the bad, the characteristics we dream about in our "perfect" man, mate, and partner; and the deal breakers, too. Those "perfect" qualities don't always add up to Mr. Right. Look instead for someone who makes you a better person, someone who makes you want to get up in the morning and say hello, or jump into bed at night to cuddle. Most of all look for someone who respects you RIGHT NOW, not who will love you when you land a more fabulous job or when you become the person who you want to be in the future. Your ideal man may not even have one trait on that list you made in high school. That's okay; in fact, that's just fine, because, you know what? You're not the same person you were back then, either.

A woman I know professionally (a nurse at my doctor's office) was widowed before she turned forty. Her husband died a slow death from an awful hereditary disease. Janet knew long before her husband passed away that they would not spend the rest of their lives together. Even so, after he passed away she looked for someone who was just like him—handsome, smart, nice family, loads of money. Nobody she met measured up. Then she stopped looking. What happened next was both predictable (he was a patient of the doctor in the adjacent office) and unexpected.

Her new beau, now husband, was the complete opposite of her first husband—older, not particularly good looking and by no stretch of the imagination "cute," no family pedigree. On the other hand, he was funny, kind, and a good provider. What he lacked in looks and family money he made up for with vitality, patience, and a sense of adventure. Janet thought her hopes for "Mr. Right" had died when she buried her first husband. Every day she thanks her lucky stars she did not let her "ideal" get in the way of her second chance for happiness.

Value Your Values

Know yourself and what's important to you. Know the person you are and the person you want to be in a new relationship. Do you want someone who can support you so that you don't have to work one day? Are you dreaming of a partner who will inspire you to be a better version of who you are right now? Do you just want to laugh your days away? Or maybe you require all of the above.

Barbara, a woman I met on my travels overseas, is an interesting example of the Value Your Values credo. She had been divorced for several years when I met her, but was in a year-old serious relationship when we met in Italy. "It took me a long time to figure out that if I was going to be in a good relationship again it would have to be with someone who had wanderlust and who wanted to travel as much as I do," she explained. Barbara had an Internet marketing company and could serve clients from anywhere, as long as she had her laptop and access to Wi-Fi. "That meant I could do my job from wherever I wanted. But for years I talked myself into believing I needed to date a guy with a desk job. How ridiculous is that? If I am going to be in a relationship, I want to actually be in the relationship. And I am not going to put off my travel plans to wait for a corporate guy to take his three-week vacation."

When Barbara decided to stop waiting and start traveling

(working along the way) solo, she hooked up with ex-pats on her journeys through Europe, the Far East, and Africa. "The great thing about international travel in the Internet age is that it's easy to find ex-pat groups everywhere, including single ex-pat groups," she says, recommending *International Living* magazine (and Web site) as a good resource for such information. It was in one of these ex-pat groups where she met Howard, her new partner. He's a photographer and writer, who makes his living capturing far-flung places and people around the globe, in pictures and words. "We suit each other and we obviously share a passion for travel," she says.

Follow Barbara's lead, and be true to what you want in a partner, and honor it. Be honest with yourself about your needs and desires as the person you are today.

Stay You—Stay Me

I once dated a man who said I made him chew too fast, and when he chewed "too fast" food came up into the back of his throat. Confession: I have a tendency to speak very quickly, and this would make him nervous. Despite the fact he thought I was amazing and we had a fabulous time together, when we ate together, I essentially made him ill. He would say, "It's not you, it's me." "Damn right," I would think, but I really liked him and thought he had all the traits that I thought were ideal for me. So to please him I stopped talking when we ate. Yep, imagine that. Eat, drink, be merry . . . but please don't say anything.

It wasn't until I looked up one day and got real with myself: the fact was, he was not the right guy for me, and an unconscious part of me knew that. I realized I was being passive-aggressive by my all-or-nothing response to his digestive tic. Never once did it occur to me simply to talk more slowly. I came up with a more drastic, and ultimately unsustainable, solution that enabled me to realize that we were going to be that couple that sits together but doesn't speak together. That drifts off looking past each other or worse, at the newspaper while slowly chewing our food so that it stays down. We parted ways. I learned a valuable lesson about myself, though: I am who I am, and I cannot change that for anyone. You are you—and this lesson applies to you, too. Stay you. Not him.

That said, as long as we are talking about what *you* really want, let's talk about what *men* really want. This section is not meant to suggest you should throw out all you have learned and conform for a man. It's not so that you learn the perfect way to play games. And, it's not for you to become someone you are not. Yes, I know, you want to be yourself. And you can be.

Here are a few ways to ensure that you are not wasting time on the dating scene wondering what happened and stalking his social media pages to see where he's gone. Take these tips or leave them. Take a few or take them all.

The New Single . . . Rules
#1 Why Hasn't He Called?

I wrote an entire book about this subject and I stand by these words: if he hasn't called—he's not interested. Bottom line. End of discussion. But just in case you don't agree with me, I will elaborate. If a man doesn't call, you are not on his mind. It's pretty cut and dry. Think about it; when you call a friend you are thinking about her. It's that simple. There are men out there who are players, but most men don't play games. There is a big difference. If he likes you, he is going to call when he asks for your number.

If he is not worried about you and just kind of interested, you will hear from him on his own time.

A friend of mine who lives in LA has been my resource for years on dating. She is fifty-five, in great shape, and has a great business. A class act. Should be easy for her to find a guy—right? Wrong. She is too pushy. If a man doesn't call her after he says he is going to, she calls him. Her call may yield her a second date, but it guarantees she doesn't get a third. The same holds true whether we are talking about a man who has never been married or a man who is back out on the dating scene. They want to call you. And it may take them three weeks to do so. So what? If they don't, move on.

#2 He's Not Your Bestie

You have been through a lot, but a new man does not automatically become your best friend. As women we often find ourselves saying words like, "I don't want to play games," or "I want him to be my best friend." That is perfectly fine. No one is telling you to play games. But what I am telling you is to play it right. Earlier in the book we spoke about self-care and self-love. I included therapy in that section. It is not because I think you need to run to a shrink every time you have a problem, but I do believe it is important to have a sounding board as you go through this next stage of your life. *Don't* use a guy as your best friend, your therapist, or your confidant. He wants to be an equal partner. He wants to be in your life. Men don't want to take over your life or feel like you can't be without them. Keep your relationships and your boundaries intact and don't cross the streams.

3 He Doesn't Want a Mother

The first time a guy said this to me I was horrified. I was cleaning up the dishes from the meal I had cooked him. I offered dessert, and then proceeded to dish it out to him. I ran and got him another fork. I filled up his coffee and I got him a napkin. I am somewhat embarrassed to admit that when I brought him the napkin, I used it to wipe a little smudge at the corner of his mouth. The next night when I asked him about why he was being so cool to me, he said, "Tamsen, I am not looking for a mother." I couldn't believe my ears. I thought I was being kind and attentive and caring and nurturing, but I realized to my horror I *was* trying to be his mother.

As a woman who doesn't have children of her own, I often find myself taking people under my wing or being too attentive. Even if you have children—try to keep this in mind. He doesn't want a mother. He wants a woman. A partner. A lover. If you find yourself cutting up his food, nurturing him too much, fretting around him, or picking up his toys—I mean clothes—stop immediately. Or adopt a dog.

And by the way, if he reacts positively to your mothering . . . um, do you really want to have a "son" who is your age or older? Loving your mothering is a red flag, ironically. Lisa, a friend from Philadelphia, had a somewhat comical experience like this— which she luckily got out of before it was too late. "I did what you did," she told me, "and I sort of catered to the guy a little too much in the beginning because he was good-looking and I thought I liked him." Anyway, it turns out Lisa's guy took to her mothering skills a little too well. "One Sunday I actually stopped myself in front of the dryer and realized, I was doing this guy's laundry, which he was planning on picking up later that day. And we didn't even have a date planned." It wasn't long after that, that Lisa pulled the plug on that relationship. And she finally had her washer and dryer to herself again.

#4 Deal With His Habits or Move On

You are not going to change a man. Slurping coffee. Chewing too loudly. Leaving up the toilet seat. Forgetting every little thing you tell him. You may alter his behavior, or he may adjust what he does in front of you to avoid issues, but you are not going to change him. If you are looking to do that so that he is "perfect" or at least not driving you crazy, you must realize that even if he changes those habits temporarily, he will go back to who he was or is. Remember the fellow who objected to the way I talked? Would you like it, or would you feel resentful? Even if he thinks that he is helping you be a better version of yourself, you would feel angry about it. Eventually you would revert back to who you were and where you are comfortable. His habits are his habits. Love them and him or leave him. Don't try to change him.

#5 Talk Like a Lady

I am a big fan of Steve Harvey, actor, entertainer, television/radio personality, and author of *Act Like a Lady, Think Like a Man*. I think he is the real deal when it comes to talking to the ladies about men. But if I were to add something to his line "Act like a lady, think like a man," I would add "Talk like a lady." I have found that so many men are not interested in having a drinking buddy to hang with on their days off. It's fine to share his interests, and if you want to sit and watch a game with him or go to your favorite beer garden, I'm all in. But make sure and maintain who you are as a lady. A man wants someone to act like a lady, and also talk like one. Keep the cursing to a minimum. Let him scream and yell with his friends. I am not saying you can't have a good time, I am saying let him have his fun friends and let him have his fun date. You don't have to be both to him.

I recently met a tall, gorgeous doctor who was in her mid-thirties. She looked more like a model than a plastic surgeon; nevertheless, she had the whole package. But, because she felt she intimidated men she would work hard to be "one of the guys" on the weekends with the men she dated. Eventually she had a whole lot of male friends but no real prospects. She would curse at the television and drink beer with the boys, but they would eventually go be with their lady friends. And she was alone. Have fun, but don't be the life of the party at your own expense.

#6 Keep Away From the Numbers Game

You know what I am talking about. You have asked him "the question." We all have. It's almost impossible not to. But despite your deep-rooted curiosity and desire to know how many women he has been with, who he has been with, where, when, why, and how long—don't ask. Just don't. You know deep in your heart if the guy is a player. You know whether or not you are being played if you listen to your gut. Go with it. Be safe. Don't be silly. But keep away from the numbers game. It is the question men hate and, quite frankly, one that most women hate as well. If you are with a guy who is turning the tables and asking you the same question, you need to respond in a way that is classy but not specific. You can answer with a response that says, I have been with men, I won't lie, but I am not worried about what was in the past, I am looking to the future. I was safe, and that is just about all he need know.

#7 Take Off Your Reporter's Hat

I have talked to men who say many first dates feel like job interviews. Or worse, an inquisition. I admit that I do have my fair share of questions when I sit across the table from someone, but - as hard as it is, I try to respect the fact that no one can be authentic if they are being scrutinized. A first date can be stressful for both parties, so try to get your answers without making him feel there is a light shining above his head asking him a barrage of questions that must be answered before the main course. Let things come out in time and, not only will you get an answer, more often than not you will get a genuine one.

Judy, a savvy colleague of mine, says she gets valuable information she is curious about by asking follow-up questions to things her date has volunteered. "I want to show I am a good listener, and one of the best ways to do that is ask a question that demonstrates you heard what he just said and you're interested in it." Men love to talk about themselves (hey, I'm being honest!), and by letting them lead the conversation in the beginning means you can lead it even further by responding to what they say. Judy's strategy is right on. As a journalist, I know that people offer up more information when they believe the person they are talking to is genuinely interested in what they are saying. That ego stroking encourages them to carry on.

#8 Don't Tie One On

When it comes to drinking—know your limit. There is nothing pretty about what I call "white wine breath." I know you want to be fun. We all do. A little more wine than usual can help make you seem like the fun girl you think you should be. I have talked to so many men who are turned off by the girl who drinks too much then tries desperately to act like she is not actually drunk or tipsy or silly. A woman I worked with a few years ago, Alicia, came to me for advice on getting back into the dating world. As an eternal optimist, she signed up for every dating site out there. You name it, she paid the monthly membership fees to be on it. "Plenty of Fish" got her time as well, since she followed any site that advertised along the sides of the paid sites. She was looking for love not in all the wrong places, but in any place she could find to look for it.

I am not against putting yourself out there, but do so only after you have become secure in your New Single self. Alicia was trying to find herself by finding a man, and as a result she went out with one guy after another. I am all for dating a lot of men, but it was clear that most of the guys she met were just looking for one thing. Because she was still not clear who she was, and had not dated for a long time, the minute she got their attention, she said thank you by jumping into bed with them—generally after having a few too many drinks.

We are not talking about a promiscuous woman here. We are simply talking about a woman who drank too much on each date because she was not comfortable. She got comfortable. Then, she got too comfortable. It took endless nights of asking herself, "Why hasn't he called?" until she finally came to terms with the fact that she had no choice but to learn her limit and make the guy fall for her instead of her falling all over him, drunk.

#9 Shop for Your Labels—Don't Ask Him for One

I know this sounds cute. It's meant to. But it's serious. Very serious. Most men want to head for the hills when you ask the dreaded "Where do we stand?" question. Those are scary words for most men. You will find the occasional one who is not put off, but overall most men like to let things happen in time. Especially if you are back out there dating men who have probably just gone through the same thing you have. You do not need a label right now on your relationship. What's the point? If you have to ask him for one, then you don't really have one. If a guy wants to see just you, you will know it. If he doesn't, you will know it. If he's not saying it, assume he is seeing other women, until such time as you know it for sure.

HOW TO PICK A DARING FIRST DATE PLACE

Wine breath. I have referenced it above. I hate it. I am sure we have all had it, but I cannot imagine a bigger turnoff to either party on a date than wine breath or being somewhat sloppy when going out the first time. So, I wanted to take a moment and find some alternative places to meet someone new "for drinks." The point of a first date is to allow for conversation . . . good conversation. So, if you dare to be daring on a first date, here are a few suggestions to try:

1. Bowling—yes, it's old-school. Way old-school. But it's trendy and there is a cool kind of fun vibe to it that allows you to take your guard down and just have fun.

2. Art Gallery—you don't have to be snotty to head to your local art gallery. It can be fun, inexpensive, and you actually have the chance to walk around and talk. Isn't that the point?

3. Music Venue—one of the most fun dates I ever went on for a first date was Blue Note jazz club down in the Village. It was fun. Period. We didn't work out, but I enjoyed the night, the conversation between sets, and greatly respected the fact he was daring enough to try something different for a first date.

4. Tourist for a Day—there is nothing I love more than acting like a tourist in the city I love. I am sure there are places you have never even been in your own city. Why not explore them with someone new. I am not so familiar with all parts of downtown—for a first date, walking the streets of the East Village is always fun, or stopping for coffee. Or dinner if it looks like the night is going well.

5. Daring New Place—we all have our tried-and-true restaurants that make us feel safe on a first date, but why not be daring. Try a place neither of you have been to. Maybe a place where you cook on the table in front of you or go for a fondue desert—you get to explore and you get to explore someone's personality at the same time.

#10 Leave the *L* Word to Him

Just because he is nice to you, it doesn't mean he is in love with you. At a time when we are rebuilding ourselves, it's easy to feel vulnerable and seek out people who are kind to us. Let the love come in time. Hearing the words "I love you" are not as important as feeling them. Allow him to fall in like with you first; in the long run, that strong foundation of fondness means so much more to a man who is looking for love. In order for a relationship to really sustain the test of time, both people must truly *like* each other in order to love each other.

Real Men Lead From Behind

The funny and interesting thing about bad relationships is that, in retrospect, they are made up of a series of missed metaphors. When, in hindsight, maybe all I needed was a simile.

So, once I was lost in Arles, France. Not really lost, but definitely not found. I was sightseeing with the Professor. Ironically, he told me to buy a map. I dutifully followed the order, heading into a store to make the purchase. When I stepped back out, he was gone. Remember that story I told about being lost in a department store for an eternity, looking for Mom and Dad? This was the adult equivalent of that moment. Wandering the streets of a foreign country without a familiar face in sight can be terrifying.

I'm a free spirit. I am headstrong. Full steam ahead, all the time, no matter where I or we are going, even when I have no idea where I or we are going. Basically, I like to feel like I'm in charge. At least, I like to feel like I'm in charge until it's blatantly obvious that I have no idea what's happening. I was a child lost in a department store all over again. Panic. Sweat. Wild-eyed terror.

And then, there he was again. "Where the hell have you been?" I blasted at him. To which he responded, "I knew you could take care of yourself." Maybe I could; maybe I couldn't. Either way, why would he leave me to have a nervous breakdown?

This was the same man who would dart across the street as the light would change, only to leave me behind, stumbling in front of moving cars, in my five-inch heels. This was the same man who refused to help me carry the groceries around the store because the crowd made him irritated. This was the same man who would make a run for the subway, even if it meant me missing the train and him making it. I was lost and I had no idea how to get found.

Let's rewind back to more words, thoughts, and actions of wisdom from my father. As I said, I like to feel like I'm in charge. That's why my dad and I are such a great team; in any sort of relationship, he believes in leading from behind.

Don't know what that means? It's the Nelson Mandela axiom, from his 1994 autobiography, *Long Walk to Freedom*. A leader, he wrote, is like a shepherd. "He stays behind the flock, letting the most nimble go out ahead, whereupon the others follow, not realizing that all along they are being directed from behind."

My father always said he was leading from behind. Like so many of his pearls of wisdom, I didn't know what he meant until I actually needed to. If, like me, you're headstrong but secretly vulnerable, the next time you find yourself ready for love, look for someone who leads from behind—not someone who barrels ahead and leaves you behind.

Real Men Don't Dither

I get a lot of questions from women who are dating again after a long relationship, and they are trying to figure out who the guy is. They are successful, smart, and savvy. Women on top. But time and time again these fabulous femme fatales get messed up inside about guys who are confirmed bachelors or not "sure" where things stand. Here is the painful truth none of us wants to hear: if a man wants to be with you, really be with you, he will be. He will be upfront. He will be clear. He will not leave his feelings up for your interpretation. It will not require nights of endless conversation, questions, confusion, or talks about where things stand or where we are going.

A Keeper . . .

- Will be clear as to what he wants.

- He will respect who you are and what you want.

- He will take things at your pace.

- Will not be afraid of commitment. Or if he is, he will be honest about it.

- He will be single. He will not be "sort of single," "separated," or "married but they have an understanding."

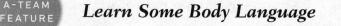

A-TEAM FEATURE   *Learn Some Body Language*

It's not always enough to go by what people say, that's why I talked with Tonya Reiman, a renowned body language expert who shared some insight on what certain body language can tell you.

WHAT CAN YOU LEARN FROM A PERSON'S BODY LANGUAGE?

Everyone you know has made at least one major mistake because they trusted the wrong person, so wouldn't it be great to learn a technique that could protect you from the liars of the world? This technique is called "baselining." Baselining is detecting an individual's deceit signals by first detecting their truth signals. Put simply, a truth signal is an individual's normal behavior when not under pressure or trying to "sell" themselves.

How does the person stand? What is the position of his trunk and torso? Does he orient toward or away from you? Does he use high gestures or lower gestures? What is his neutral facial expression? Does he maintain eye contact while he speaks? How often does he blink?

Finally, what is his normal eye position when speaking, and remember—does he look up, down, or to the side; does he look left or right? Note these signals and when engaging with this individual, if you notice several deviations, these are red flags and should be examined. Keep in mind, you need to look for clusters of clues; sometimes people scratch their face simply because it is itchy.

WHAT ARE SOME OF THE COMMON SIGNALS FOR DECEIT?

These behaviors are not foolproof barometers of deception, they enhance your ability to pick up on reactions and then compare the verbals to the nonverbals to ensure they are in sync. Keep in mind, there are times when people use the same behaviors merely to relieve or reduce stress based on their current circumstances.

1. Increase in blink rate

Liars tend to blink more as lying usually causes stress. Under stress, eye blink rate increases as the cognitive overload of deception causes less conscious attention to eye blink rate and more attention to maintaining the lie.

2. Sudden increase or decrease in gestures

When lying, the sympathetic nervous system, which controls involuntary expression, can become aroused and lead to an increase in movements. Conversely, the person may become so fearful of being caught in the lie that they go on body language lockdown and show no movement whatsoever.

3. Use of nondominant hand for emphasis

When we are deceptive, quite often, we do not feel passionate about our statements. This will shine through when someone chooses to make a passionate gesture with their nondominant hand.

4. Hand-to-face gestures

When individuals lie they tend to bring their hand to their face for several reasons. They might scratch their nose (when we become anxious the capillaries in our noses slightly expand, making our noses itch), they might rub their eyes (this allows them to break eye contact and gives them a moment to gather new thoughts), perhaps they cover their mouth (at times we go back to childhood with the belief that covering our mouth allows the lie to be invisible).

5. Change in their visual access cues

Thinking requires specific areas of the brain to be accessed. Typically when we are remembering something we will look up, down, or to the side as well as looking off to the left or right. If you take a second to watch where a person looks when he is obviously remembering something, note if that direction changes during the course of your conversation. If he is looking in the other direction, he may be attempting to fabricate his answer.

6. Dupers delight

There are people who absolutely enjoy telling a lie— for these individuals, you may notice that immediately following their deception, the corners of their mouth upturn. This is an unconscious movement, which betrays their sincerity and conveys that they are happy to have pulled one over on you.

7. The shoulders move either individually or together

If the person you are speaking to gives an affirmative statement while shrugging one or both shoulders, he is not 100 percent certain of his answer. This is the body's way of admitting there is conflict between the words and his belief. We see this often in politicians who make promises they probably cannot or will not keep. The words say yes, the shoulders say, "I don't know."

8. Tongue protrusion or lip swiping

Typically individuals who feel that guilty about lie do this. They will either push their tongue out in disgust as if they were eating something distasteful or they will swipe their lips from one side to the other, mentally wiping away their deception.

9. Self-pacification gestures

When we become nervous about lying we tend to rub and touch ourselves more in an effort to create comfort. Rubbing different parts of the body (neck, legs, arms, etc.) stimulates nerve endings, which releases endorphins into the brain, making us feel better.

10. Word usage

Liars tend to avoid statements of ownership. Instead of something being "mine" it is "ours." They will also use distancing language such as the word "the." "The" car instead of "my" car. In addition, people who are being deceptive tend to use more negative words as they are typically more anxious and the guilt they feel induces pessimistic language.

SINGLE
FAB
FEMALE

Date Night Tips

I am a far from a fashionista. I love fun dresses. I love bargain shopping. And I love fun colors. So the advice for Date Night may not be what's on trend right now, but it is what I think works for a more classic look so that you feel comfortable and don't look like someone you are not.

1. Natural

I know that guys say they like a "natural" look, but I do caution against heading to drinks with bed head and no mascara.

2. Simple Elegance

Dress so that you are comfortable, but not too comfortable. I have talked to so many guys who love a girl that is able to show up for a date in jeans, nice white shirt, and wedges. There is something attractive about less is more. I happen to be a dress girl, so I always go for a classic A-line dress paired with wedge heels and understated accessories such as hoop earrings and a pendant—simple, easy, and I don't have to worry about matching!

3. All About the Eyes

You don't have to have smoky eyes for a casual drink date or coffee, but make sure your eyes look bright and alert!

- Moisturize

- Use mascara—I never leave home without it

- Add some individual lashes if you are a little bare in that department—I opt for the ones that come off at night

- Line your eyes but don't go overboard; you don't want to look like a raccoon

4. Play It Loose

Don't wear anything skintight. No one wants to sit across the table watching you pull at your neckline or hips all night long. Make sure you have worn the outfit before so you know how it fits and that you feel good in it.

5. Heels

I am addicted to shoes. All kinds and shapes and sizes and especially ones with big heels. If you are a pro at walking in heels, go nuts. But if you are doing it to look sexy and can barely stand up in them—pass on the heels and be safe!

6. *Tone Down the Smell*
    Perfume is great. A light spritz is great. Don't overdo it.

Boomer Style, Great Style

Sherrie Mathieson is a former movie stylist and a fashion and grooming consultant now based in Scottsdale, Arizona. She is also the author of two books, *Forever Cool* and *Steal This Style*. Sherrie offers some really hardworking 4-1-1 on how boomer women, who may have been out of the dating world for some time, should think about their personal style when out and about and meeting men.

WHAT ARE SOME OF THE COMMON STYLE/ GROOMING MISTAKES NEWLY SINGLE BOOMER-AGED WOMEN MAKE WHEN THEY ARE TRYING TO GET BACK INTO THE DATING/MEETING MEN SCENE?

The biggest mistake is dressing too sexy or inappropriately "young," belying insecurity about her desirability—instead of choosing simplicity and understatement with modern style that says "youthful" yet ageless—that projects self-assurance. With grooming the goal should be "approachable" and "less is more."

Naturalness (you can still use subtle makeup) and a healthy appearance is always appealing.

HOW DOES A BOOMER WOMAN ASSESS HER WARDROBE—WHICH COULD PROBABLY USE SOME REFRESHING AFTER A BREAKUP OR DIVORCE?

This is highly individual. If a woman neglected herself (also possibly her figure) and her wardrobe—she would do well to reassess. Think "healthy vanity" in your new pursuit. Fit is so important, as is working with colors that flatter. What is modern, rather than merely trendy? A fresh approach requires perusal of high-end magazines, Web sites, and visiting upscale stores to see choices. Consider not buying as much black anymore as it becomes harsh-looking except on women with dark complexions. If she needs a style consultant to help, she should seek out a *good one* (not a store's personal shopper or salesperson—as they are not neutral). Hair (flattering, shiny, and not stiff or rigid style), nails (not chipped, too flashy, too long, or with "French" chalky white nail tips), and makeup may need attention to be current and attractively healthy-looking. The more natural the effect—the better! Eyeglasses may need updating . . . some styles read (pun intended:) "old."

WHAT ARE SOME KEY PIECES SHE SHOULD HAVE IN HER WARDROBE? WHAT NEW THINGS SHOULD SHE INVEST IN?

Here's my go-to must-have list of no-fail items:

- White and dark navy jeans—straight and narrow (bootleg with heels or platforms still work, too)

- White polo shirt

- Denim shirt

- Languid mid-thigh-length gray sweater

- Pair of driving moccasins

- "Chanel"-style ballerina shoe

- Navy/white sailor stripe top with three-quarter sleeve

- Tunic top

- Pair of knee-high flat boots and a pair with heels

- Navy shirt and a white shirt

- Black, navy, or gray "pencil" knee-length skirt

- Black patent, kitten-heeled pointy-toe pump

- Simple knee-length dress

- An "investment" bag

- Think in terms of neutral tones like tans, beiges, browns, and whites (but eschewing black, which ages boomer women)

- Gray is a great color (50 shades at least!)

- Well-chosen "Statement" jewelry especially in sterling

- A six-ply pashmina shawl in gray or navy, or a blue-red

- Short trench coat

- Modern, simple down winter jacket or coat

- Add an orange accent piece to your wardrobe. Can be a scarf, bracelet, or even a purse.

- Find a beautiful short sweater—dressy enough to go with sleeveless dresses (hard to find!)

WHAT IS THE RIGHT "LOOK" FOR A CASUAL AFTERNOON LUNCH DATE; AN AFTERWORK COCKTAIL DATE; AND A MORE FORMAL DINNER AND THEATER DATE?

This is a broad topic depending on "where" . . . and the season. Fit is critical—not too tight, revealing, or too loose.

CASUAL LUNCH:

- A mid-thigh-length gray sweater over a fresh white tank, a silver cuff bracelet, silver mid- to larger-size or very tiny hoop earrings (or pearl/diamond studs)

- White jeans

- Tan patent driving moccasins

- Navy Goyard tote

AFTERWORK COCKTAILS:

- The same sweater over a white shirt

- Paired with a gray pencil skirt

- Large-size pearl sixteen-inch necklace or silver jewelry

- Kitten-heeled or higher black patent pumps or sling-backs

- The Goyard bag or another bag in black patent

FORMAL DINNER DATE:

- A white, gray, or navy simple modern, knee-length sheath dress. Not too revealing. Pick one in the best fabric you can afford.

- The same pearl necklace

- A short jacket or sweater (the one that is hard to find) or a sumptuous shawl (never just two-ply)

- Black patent heels but perhaps with a 3½-inch heel

- A small complementary bag (clutch or on a chain)

SINGLE
FAB
FEMALE

Making Up

I am a girlie girl when it comes to makeup. I don't wear much if I am not at work, but I do have some key items with me at all times. I learned how to do my makeup from Diane Pottinger, NYC makeup artist, who has made it her mission to do more with less. If you are out, here are her must-haves-with-you at all times.

> **1.** Concealer—banish those dark marks under the eye. A little goes a long way.
>
> **2.** Mascara—it opens up your eyes and you can keep layering for a sultry look.
>
> **3.** Lip Gloss—not too dark, but the right color can be a girl's best friend.

You *Are the Prize*

About a year and a half after my divorce was official my family decided to have a reunion. Lovely. It was the first time my family had ever had one—go figure. Nevertheless, I was "between boys" and decided that this was going to be a time to get to know the family members I had not seen in years. I am originally a Texas girl and, true to my roots, we decided the Riverwalk in San Antonio would be a good halfway point for a lot of my older relatives. Bright and early Saturday morning I hit the Lone Star State as the New Single of the Fadal family.

Often we forget who makes up our extended family when we get busy day after day, but when I arrived at the hotel and went down to meet everyone the first night, I ran into my cousin. She is actually my second cousin, but was always the one my parents said I looked like when I put on a little too much red lipstick. I was excited to see her. She, like me, had been in the media business for a long time and she always seemed to have great stories. She was a strong woman. And, by the way, single, seventy, and still sexy.

Pretty good start to the weekend. As the night went on, I found myself telling Donna about the guy I was dating. I said he was simply perfect, but he was going "through a lot" right now and just needed some time. We had gone on trips together. He spent weeks at a time with me (we live in separate states). We talked five times a day. He was not seeing anyone else and neither was I, but he wasn't WITH me either.

Donna is from Texas. The heart of Texas. She is one of those Southern women that men just love and women want to be like. I also happen to be from Texas, but never quite developed her degree of Southern charm. So here I was making excuses for the man I was sure was my soul mate; my Southern belle cousin turned to me and said in her fabulous Texas drawl, "Honey, you are the prize. There is nothing else to talk about." I thought, yes, yes, I understand, but he is going through so much right now and he is great and we travel together, and . . . and . . . and. As I listened to my own unconvincing words, I kept repeating to myself—you are the prize. Was I? Where had I lost my self-confidence? When did I think it was okay to accept mediocre when I was giving 1,000 percent?

If you have to chase a man, bend over backward to accommodate his schedule, or change your plans or your persona to be with him and be a part of his life—you are not a part of his life at all. You are simply convenient. As a New Single, you had better start thinking about what you want to be. Do you want to simply be with someone because it's convenient to him? Or do you want to be with someone because he treats you right and really wants to be with you?

I have been the convenience. It sucks.

This is the time to let go of that dead-end relationship and find someone who is excited to be with you. Find someone who is not stringing you along until he finds someone who is right for him. Chances are, he is not even looking for anyone because he

is a confirmed bachelor or simply too selfish. But as long as he is
in your life, there is not room for anyone else. It hurts. It feels
bad. And, it feels empty, but not forever. Be true to yourself.

Lessons From Smart Women

"I conquered the SUNDAY. I think Sundays are the hardest day in the week for singles, couples and families everywhere. I have learned how to have great Sundays. You get
out of the house and face it head on. You find a favorite
place or thing for YOU on Sunday and you experience it.
Don't hide at home with work or old movies. Learning to
live in your own skin takes time . . . and caring for yourself
first—any day of the week—isn't selfish, it's survival . . . and
it leads to such growth. Now, I have the company of men
when I want . . . I'm lucky. But I love the company of me
first—on any Sunday I like."
—Trish Rubin, NYC Brand Management Consulting

Will He Make a Good Father?

While I don't have children myself, I do have a furry child who
is the little love of my life. I bring this up, because even how a
man reacts to a seven-pound Chihuahua can give you some insight into how he is going to be as a man or a father or simply a
person.

In this case, my "Professor Higgins" was tall, dark, and handsome. He was the man I was certain I would spend the rest of

my life with because I thought I had lost him the first time around (yes, he is the guy from the introduction of this book). Once we starting dating after my divorce, we felt comfortable with him coming to stay with me in New York. My apartment had been scrubbed of my ex and it was mine again, and I was the New Single.

Unfortunately, there were no books out there on how to deal with a man whom I had suddenly found out refused to be in the same room as a dog. He didn't have allergies. It certainly had not been a point of conversation because we would often travel together. When he said he was "not a dog person," I figured he was a cat person and left it at that. Little did I know that he literally had a visceral reaction to the mere mention of dogs. So much, in fact, that when he came to New York, he would not come if my dog was at my apartment. Luckily, my ex loves our dog as much as I do and was willing to take him for the week that the Professor would be here.

It gave me that sick feeling in my stomach, but as a lot of women do, I pushed it down and said, in time, he will adjust, if it's important to me, he will learn how to deal with my little furry kid. He doesn't have to let the dog sleep in bed, but he will allow me to have my dog. Time came and went. That never happened. I realized this was one of those signs that we should not ignore. It was a sign that said, I love myself, but what you love is not as important to me. With that, the man went and the dog stayed.

Whether you have children already, furry children, or you want to have children in the future with a man, you need to make sure he would make a good father. There is no perfect science to this, but as we often change the flags from RED to PINK, here are some things you can look at and look for to determine if he is a dad-ready guy:

1. He wants to meet your children.

2. He does not wince when you bring up your children or bring up having children.

3. He listens when your child talks to him.

4. He respects his child's mother if he has children already.

5. He is interested in how your child is doing in school or after-school activities.

6. He is good with kid-friendly outings and wants to have your children along.

7. He has fun with your children or his own, but he also understands the balance of being fun and firm if they need to be reprimanded.

8. He is not threatening or physical with the children if they misbehave.

9. He is prepared and willing financially to take care of you and your kids.

10. He does not get hysterical if your child tracks mud into his house or spills food in the car. He is patient and follows your lead when it comes to the children.

CHAPTER SEVEN

The X Factor

*"We must be willing to let go of the life
we have planned, so as to have the life
that is waiting for us."*

—E.M. FORSTER

The Moment

I had just finished working the morning show. I spent a long time being pretty tired and sleep deprived. This particular day, it was sunny and gorgeous. Still a little cool, but you could feel that summer was right around the corner. I had a few minutes to spare before meeting an old friend for lunch at the Flatiron Building, so I sat on a bench in the pedestrian walkway right near the building. My ex and I were already separated, but we were working together, talking several times a day, and in general carrying on as if we were still married because we had not filed for divorce. At that point, I knew it was inevitable but there was something about knowing he was still there that made me feel less like a failure and not so alone in the world.

I got up from where I was sitting and started to cross Fifth Avenue when I saw my ex walking along the sidewalk. It was nowhere near his office and pretty far from mine, so for him to be there was odd. He was across Fifth Avenue and walking with someone. That wasn't too unusual because he would often have lunch meetings with people for the business. His name was about to come out of my mouth when I saw him pick up the girl's hand and walk her across the street. I stopped cold. With New York traffic and sounds and people surrounding me, all I could hear was my heart beating outside my chest. I finally reached the Flatiron Building and had to hold myself up against it to breathe. I tried to call the mediator we were working with, but when she answered the phone first ring, I hung up on her because I couldn't speak.

I went to lunch and tried to put it out of my mind. Then I went home and cried. It was not just that he was walking with someone new, but there were so many feelings of finality that were difficult to put into words. I felt my heart hurting. And, I felt sad. And, I felt embarrassed. We were continuing to live together trying to make something work. In the end, I paid more emotionally and mentally. I often get similar stories from women (and men). In the end though, these are the times that make us stronger.

Ironically, things have a way of working out down the line.

The building on Fifth Avenue that was holding me up when my legs were about to go out from under me was the Flatiron Building. It happens to be the same building that St. Martin's Press is housed in. The publishing company that two years later made it possible for me to bring my message to you.

Now, nearly three years after my divorce, my ex and I co-exist in each other's life when necessary. We don't talk daily. We don't chat about our problems with each other. And, we don't go back and talk about what was or whose fault it was or what happened. It is cordial and it is civil and it doesn't take energy from me or make me feel badly. It simply exists in my life when it has to because I have accepted the X factor. The minute you do, you will realize it's for you, not for him.

DOES THERAPY WORK?

Linda Meaney, LCSW-R, a New York psychotherapist, has been dishing out good advice to New Singles for more than twenty years. Here, she answers some questions about what to expect from therapy—how it can help you and what happens during a session.

WHY GO INTO THERAPY AFTER A DIVORCE WHEN YOU FEEL EMOTIONALLY STABLE?

It's an emotionally transformative and life-changing event that is difficult even for the most emotionally grounded person to deal with. It's a major life event. In the 2010 movie *Eat, Pray, Love*, in contrast, the wife, Elizabeth Gilbert (Julia Roberts), is unhappy with her marriage and leaves her husband. She embarks on a journey of self-exploration through Italy, India, and Indonesia, gradually finding the rewards of food, prayer, and balanced love. Unfortunately, most of us who are undergoing or have just undergone divorce don't have the luxury of taking a yearlong self-reflective sabbatical in a faraway land. We need to be closer to home.

Sometimes we can turn to friends and family. But often we need the assistance of somebody trained in exploring loss, learning from it and moving on: a psychotherapist. Over 70 percent of psychotherapy is provided by licensed clinical social workers (the rest, by psychiatrists or psychologists). After completing a master's degree, psychotherapists usually receive specialized training for treating particular populations (e.g., couples, families, and children) and problems (e.g., addictions, eating disorders, and loss/grief). Most of them, however, can assist with the pain and bewilderment of separation and divorce.

How is a therapist different from a friend?

Because a psychotherapist has objectivity and training, he or she can give us impartial guidance and new insights. Some of the help will be practical: for example, even if we find divorce to be liberating, we may need advice about coping with loneliness, adjusting to a change in status, getting along with our ex in shared parental responsibilities, and finding new companionship. Some of the help may be on a deeper level: for example, in exploring how our seemingly bottomless sense of loss, even over someone whom we may no longer love, may actually be precipitated by feelings of prior losses.

How do I find the therapist who is right for me?

In the early twenty-first century, new technology makes it easier to find a therapist than previously. But many seasoned psychotherapists don't have Web sites, aren't hooked up to social media, and don't advertise. Usually, old-fashioned word-of-mouth referrals are the most reliable means of finding a good therapist. Set up an appointment for an introductory session. At that meeting, ask the therapist about his or her education and training. Usually, they're happy to share their background. After a few sessions, you'll be able to judge if you've found the right person to help you with transitioning into the new, post-divorce stage of your life.

Is it a simple matter to get to the root of your challenges?

Not really. Don't expect psychotherapy to be easy. Often the only way to feel better, at least at first, is to feel worse. You may have to undergo the difficult process of mourning, in which you may need to admit feelings of shame, face loneliness, learn new ways to care for and protect your children, overcome bitterness, articulate rage, recognize patterns that will prevent you from having similar unsuccessful marriages, and take risks to trust again. Be brave!

I have included some of Linda's wisest words to help you get out of the misery tape that might be playing over and over in your head:

- Seek support of friends and family.

- Do something physical every day, whether it's traditional exercise, Zumba, dance (tango, salsa), or sports (tennis, racquetball).

- Rescue an animal that is compatible with your lifestyle (unconditional love is amazing!).

- Join a book group or club.

- Take a class for pleasure and enrichment, or learn a language (with others) and travel to the country of origin.

- Identify a mission that means something to you. New York Cares has over 40,000 volunteers with an incredible diversity of short-term opportunities, and other cities have similar organizations. Volunteer Match.com has more in-depth ones by zip code and categories like tutoring/mentoring a youth.

- Get outside your comfort zone and book a tour of an exotic land. Tours are a good way to see very different places while meeting like-minded travelers.

- Closer to home, take a cooking class, wine tasting course, or DIY workshop.

LESSONS FROM SMART WOMEN

"The 'I'm sorry you're going through this' should be spoken on the days that lead up to the divorce. The divorce means you're going through it already . . . key word being *through*. You will get through it."

—Lisa Moreno, president and founder of stopcaidnow.org

Accepting Your Ex

Accepting the X factor is critical in moving forward, so let's talk candidly about it. He is always going to be part of your past, no matter if you think you can be friends or if you never want to see him again. It is up to you and only you if you are able or want him to be a part of your future. Accepting your ex sounds simple enough. And, it should be. But when you have feelings involved and emotions and history and possibly kids, it's not so easy. If you share children together or he helped raise your children, you may have no choice. But, *how* he remains a part of your future and a part of your future relationships is solely up to you to decide and to define.

Nice Ways to Say Bad Things

Talking trash about your ex is risky business when you're having that conversation with a hot new prospect. The newbie doesn't really want to hear how great your past relationship was. But he also doesn't want to think you're filled with furious anger. So, here are a few ways to soften the blow when describing your past partner's most serious offenses.

- If he robbed you blind or maxed out all of your credit cards, then he was **FINANCIALLY IRRESPONSIBLE**.

- If he flirted with every woman he ever met, he had **A WANDERING EYE**.

- If he irrationally accused you of sleeping around, he was **THE JEALOUS TYPE**.

- If he hated spending time out with your friends and coworkers and always wanted to stay home, you might say he was **SOCIALLY AWKWARD**.

- If he was as dumb as a bag of hammers, then he was **NOT BOOK SMART**.

Get the picture?

Don't get me wrong; I'm not suggesting you hide anything like this going into a relationship. But it's like getting into a hot bath; you ease into these conversations. Otherwise, even if you were the victim of your ex's pitfalls, you run the risk of giving the wrong impression.

Who Is He?

Let's define what the X factor really is. He is the person you were in love with. The person you were sure you were going to spend a significant amount of time with, if not a lifetime. Then as things do, it all changed. Whether it was you or him or both of you changing—it's over. So, there are some things that you are going to have to accept:

1. He doesn't owe you anything emotionally.

2. If you text, call, or need help, he is not obligated to come running. He is your ex. You have no current ties to him and he has none to you. Don't be disappointed, angry, or hurt if he is not around even in an emergency. He doesn't have to be.

3. He is officially with someone else.

Ouch. Not always a pretty line to hear. But, even women who wanted the divorce or breakup don't love to hear those words. He is walking her dog. Bringing her coffee. Helping with her children. You must accept this. Not try to find out more about it. Simply take it as a fact and work hard to focus on *you*. I know so many women who have a tough time not looking at their ex's social media sites for signs and photos and hidden messages. A close friend who went through a nasty divorce (that she wanted) was devastated when her ex-husband went on to have a new family. She was torn apart. She was looking for wedding announcements and birth announcements and wedding photos. It became some form of self-punishment for her. It was as if she was punishing herself for not staying with him.

When He Finds Love First

My ex-husband found a new girlfriend before I found a guy. It was weird that I was the one dating and he was settling down with someone (a woman who I think is pretty amazing). I used to ask myself, "How could he find love already, and here I am working all day and trying to date?"

My friend Kira was devastated when she learned her ex had moved in with another woman—so much so that the depression and anxiety that followed had a deleterious effect on her job performance and her other relationships. She was beside herself with all sorts of feelings—anger, jealousy, self-loathing, depression. Ironically, she actively sought out the information about her ex; she would never have known about the relationship had she not insisted on maintaining contact with her ex and asking about it. Of course, he told her—because he liked the drama, but also because he wanted her to know he had really moved on and so should she. Had she not maintained contact with him, a person whom she knew could not resist hurting her at any opportunity, she would not have known. Or at least Kira would not have known until she had gotten back on her feet again emotionally.

I highly recommend that in this high-tech, social media based society you make a concerted effort to avoid finding out what your ex is doing, even though it is both simple to do and hard to avoid. If you are sure you can handle knowing, congratulations. Most women can't handle the sting of finding out their ex is in a relationship—at least not for a while. If you still have feelings for him, or you are looking for a possible way to get back with him, or you are simply curious because you are certain he won't find anyone better than you, take a look at the new rules.

Just Say No—Contact

- **Don't stalk his Facebook friends or social media contacts.**

   A lot of times we "pretend" we are not looking at his Instagram or Facebook and instead peruse around his "contacts" to see whom he is in contact with or talking to, or (OMG) photographed with. It's not only taking away from the precious time that you should be creating your own amazing moments, but it is hurting the progress you are making going forward. And, it is not healthy behavior.

- **If you have kids, don't ask them for updates— it is bad for them and worse for you.**

   He is still their parent. You must respect that even if you are no longer with him. Whether it is unknowingly or unintentionally, putting your kids in the middle only hurts them. Keep your relationship with him professional when it comes to dealing with the children and don't try to pry information out of them because they will feel the pressure and feel they are being disloyal to you by being with him.

- **What he is doing is not what you are doing. Don't date because your ex is out on the town.**

   Simply put: it's not a contest between the two of you. Just because he has a date every Friday night, it doesn't mean you have to. Many times we view it as a competition, saying, "If he's out there, then I need to get out there and date again!" This is the time to do what *you* need to do for *yourself* so you are not dumping your issues on someone new.

- **Don't find an excuse to contact him.**

   Communicating is so easy these days that not doing it is harder than ever. Whether it's a phone call or a text—don't do it. It's all off-limits. When you get the urge to reach out . . . reach out to a friend instead, take a walk, or engage in any number of other distractions.

- **When you do need to talk about finances or scheduling kids or when he can visit the dog, e-mail him.**

   Don't look for an excuse to call. Keep e-mails brief, direct, and polite.

- **Keep e-mail contact limited to "as necessary" until you are truly no longer curious about what he does, whom he does it with, or when.**

   Do not e-mail your ex about anything other than the periodic business items you have to communicate about until your emotions have completely washed away. You might be able to be friends with him someday, but that day is not today.

- **Stop thinking of him as your partner.**

   I had a hard time with this one. Even though I was so angry with him, he was always the first person I would call when I was upset about anything. Rely on

your friends or write it down or talk to someone professionally, but don't lean on him. Don't make his the
first number you dial. Once you are able to stop thinking of your ex as your partner, you will better be able
to put him in the box he needs to be in. Men are much
better at doing this than women because we tend to
attach emotions to things. But once you remove the
partner label, you will accept him as a person, not a
partner.

Bottom line: If you don't talk to him, it gets easier in time. If you
do talk to him you run the risk of being disturbed by what
you are going to hear. If you remain bitter toward your ex and
you walk around with poison in your system and spitting venom
every time you hear his name or pass a place you used to go to,
you are not going to get far. You don't have to be besties, but at
some point in your life this person was special to you. This
person meant the world to you and accepting that his future
will be without you is more than healthy; it's essential.

I talk to my ex now, three years after our divorce. In fact, we
have met each other's significant others. I am not sure if we are
"friends," but we do know what is going on in each other's lives.
We did not have kids together, but we did have a business together so that kept us talking. After we had both gotten on with
our separate lives, and had started dating others, I had to ask
myself, "Why do I really want to stay friends with him?" Then
we both had to ask ourselves, "Will we be okay explaining this
friendship to future significant others?" Those are two very important questions to ask as you move forward in accepting your
ex. It is important to have boundaries in the relationship however you define it, so that you feel comfortable. Perhaps in the

future it's just as important, so that any potential partner is comfortable as well.

A former boss of mine went through a pretty ugly divorce. She didn't see it coming and was very devastated when her husband of fifteen years and father of her two kids came home to tell her he was very much in love with a younger version of her. She did a great job of not allowing it to affect her work, but she could not stop herself from digging for information about her former husband's new girlfriend and what she was all about. It became an obsession. She would scour Facebook to see what they were doing. She even saw the ring her husband gave his future bride (almost identical to the one he had given her years earlier). As if the divorce did not hurt enough, she was punishing herself daily by trying to not only accept her ex, but also justify why he had left her in the first place.

If you are not over the person you were with or you are searching for answers, being friends with him will not help you discover those answers. You will not "get closure" this way. You will need to get up and close the door yourself in order to avoid hurting in the future or spending countless hours looking for answers that may never come.

SEVEN WAYS NOT TO TRASH YOUR EX

I found that I have had to issue a few retractions from time to time when it comes to describing my exes using words that were not so becoming to a lady, especially during the more heated times of the post-breakup portion of the journey. And, the truth is, it can make any new potential man a little concerned that he could be the next victim of the string of expletives that roll off your tongue. Here are a few words that will

make you more attractive or at least courteous when it comes
to describing your ex.

1. Likable

2. Charming

3. Hardworking

4. Energetic

5. Outgoing

6. Driven

7. Ambitious

CHAPTER EIGHT

A Breakup Shouldn't Leave You Broke or Broken

"We are what we repeatedly do.
Excellence, therefore, is not
an act but a habit."

—WILL DURANT

I t was simple when my parents got married, I guess, or simpler than it seems to be today, at least.

They said, "I do." Went to the bank, opened a checking account and a savings account and life proceeded from there. There was talk about saving money. Talk about overspending. Talk about coupons. Talk about not being able to afford something. There was never talk about dividing assets—or, worse yet, assuming the debts of a marriage gone bad.

I naively assumed my ex and I would split the debts our business and our marriage had accumulated. The truth is I had neither sense nor cents when it came down to it because like so many people, I let my emotions get in the way. I agreed to things I should have never done just to get away from the fact I was getting divorced. The faster I could flee the mediator's table, the sooner the hurt would go away. I didn't let my lawyer do her job. Learn from my mistake.

Then there are the women who give up so much of their lives when they meet someone. During the course of my research for this book, I came upon a woman whom I have grown to respect and cherish. We are sisters of the same situation. That is how true bonds are formed.

Steph L. Wagner is a financial analyst and divorce strategist. She married her college sweetheart. They were together for twenty years, and had three amazing boys together. One day, her ex-everything decided that a woman with pink hair and glitter eye shadow was his new true love. Steph told me she was still financially dependent on this man. A man she had given up a six-figure salary for. A man that she had essentially given up her independence for—in exchange for raising their sons and the promise of "ever after." After reading her story, I reached out to her and told her mine. What I realized from our talk, after a lot of tears, trials, and tribulations, is that there is a way to make sense and cents of a breakup. Steph says her divorce inspired her to build her business. According to recent numbers, close to half of all first marriages end in divorce and nearly 65 percent of second marriages end the same way. She says that in most cases, divorce can be harder financially on women than men, since men still tend to be the breadwinners. More women than men also tend to take time out of the workforce to be caregivers.

Money Talks

Here are Steph Wagner's six financial steps for the newly single:

1. Finalize all financial arrangements.

Establishing the financial logistics of your divorce is only the first step. It is your responsibility to see that the terms of your settlement are executed, including, but not limited to: changing the way financial accounts are titled, transferring divided assets into new accounts, executing any necessary quitclaim deed on properties, and transferring title on personal property like cars, boats, RVs, etc. Update your tax withholdings and notify your CPA about any material changes to your deductions. If you have children, only one parent can claim them as dependents!

2. Disinherit your ex.

Prepare a new will, trusts, living wills, and/or medical directives and power of attorney. (It's creepy to think that my ex had the ability to pull the plug for a short time after we were divorced until I changed my will.) Remember to also select new beneficiaries on all retirement accounts (IRAs, 401ks, etc.) as well as insurance policies because beneficiary designations trump what you direct in your will.

3. Check your credit report.

Not only do you want to make certain there are no surprises, it is also important that you establish a list of liabilities that need to have your name or your ex's name removed from per your divorce decree. Be vigilant! Don't assume that the your ex has your back; in fact, assume he does not. There are three credit-reporting agencies: Equifax, Experian, and TransUnion. Each is obligated to provide you with a free copy of your report annually. The website CreditKarma.com will help you easily obtain the reports.

It is worth noting that if you own property together

and both names are on the mortgage, a quitclaim deed will NOT remove you from this obligation. Therefore, if the party who was awarded the house fails to make a payment, you are on the hook and your credit can be severely affected. To insure that you are entirely off the loan, it's best to have the property sold or have it stipulated in the decree that the existing mortgage be refinanced by your ex within a specific period of time. Make sure the refinancing is carried out.

4. Don't make irreversible financial decisions.

Undoing a rash decision can cost you a lot of money, and plenty of rash financial decisions have been made in the weeks and months after we have settled with our exes. Make a list of the things you feel you need to spend money on, be they significant—a new kitchen— or trivial—a new mailbox—then let the list mellow. I'm not saying that if your roof is leaking you shouldn't fix it, but I *am* saying now is not the time to install the infinity pool you've been lusting for but hubby didn't want. Cool it.

A friend of mine who lives in one of those adorable little towns along the Hudson River went through a pretty acrimonious divorce a few years ago. She'd been a stay-at-home mom to her and her husband's three kids, who were grown and out of the house when their parents called it quits. Because her marriage had lasted a long time, by law she was entitled to a portion of her husband's pension benefits and his social security. She also got the house on the Hudson free and clear and a reasonably generous settlement—which she promptly divided with her children (to help them pay off their college loans) and used the remainder to rent and stock the gourmet specialty store she'd long dreamed of owning.

She opened her store in October 2007, just in time for Thanksgiving and Christmas. Great timing, she thought. Not exactly. When the Great Recession began in December of that same year, sales faltered. The store was a little jewel filled with wonderful delicacies—that seemed just a little too decadent to shoppers who'd just watched one-third of their net worth evaporate overnight. My friend's lack of retail experience ("Hey, I can shop—that means I can sell") and her awful bad luck in timing meant that her portion of the settlement money was gone when the store folded a few months into the new year.

Permanently. Thirty cans of French duck confit will not pay the electric bill. As Amanda Steinberg, founder of DailyWorth, says, starting a business can be a great way to build wealth, but it's also very difficult. "Businesses eat money and it can take two years before things pop and you start making any money." Unfortunately, my friend didn't have Amanda's insights when she opened her shop and invested all her money in stocking it.

5. Think strategically.

Be strategic about the money you must spend in this early period after the divorce. If you really need cash, don't rush to liquidate your retirement accounts! The cost is simply too high. Not only are there penalties and tax consequences, you are sabotaging all the work your money has done to *build your net worth*. A better option may be to open a line of credit (home equity, personal, or business) where the terms are much more advantageous than that of a credit card (4.86% vs. 15.57% APR.)

6. Equip yourself with the right team.

Your new life deserves a strong footing and often, surrounding yourself with a new CPA, trust attorney, and financial advisor is essential. It is critical that all three share your values and ideals and possess a strong desire to work with you and the other members of your team to preserve your income, protect your assets, and build your net worth.

Becoming newly single is never easy even under the best of circumstances. And while your ex may not intentionally try to sabotage you, there are essential steps you need to take to not only protect yourself, but also create a strong financial foundation for the next chapter of your life. Your future depends on you!

A-TEAM FEATURE   *Get Clear About Money*

Amanda Steinberg is the founder of DailyWorth.com, the one-stop resource for women and their money. She's also a mom and a New Single. I read DailyWorth.com religiously. It is a resource for my financial life and for my future. Amanda has some great advice for women. Here is what she had to say to me.

IS THERE A COMMON THEME AROUND DIVORCED WOMEN AND MONEY?

Yes. Not understanding how to manage money. Women are retiring with 20 percent less than men, and to compound matters,
our collective net worth is down 36 percent and wealth inequal-
ity is growing. We have no choice but to learn how to manage
our money. My own single mom told me, "No matter what happens to you, take care of yourself and build your own wealth."
As a result of that advice, and my own independent streak, I became a maniacal entrepreneur, obsessed with earning as much
as I could. By the age of thirteen, I had learned computer programming and earned forty dollars an hour at my first job. By
the time I was twenty-five I was making two hundred thousand
a year as a programmer. Sounds good, right? It wasn't. I was paying my mortgage one day, and realized I had no money in my account. How could that be when I was thirty years old and
making more than two hundred grand a year? Money management was the missing element. Although I did not spend money
on clothing, dinners out, and so on, I had created a lifestyle well
above my head.

HOW DO WE DO THAT?

First of all, never build a life that you could not maintain on your
own. Even though I had a prenuptial agreement, I still depended
on my husband's wealth to create the lifestyle we had, including
the kind of house we lived in, private schools, and so on, while we
were married. I thought, wrongly, that I could calculate those
things into my cost and level of living after we broke up. I pay 90
percent of child care, and even though I have a successful business,

I cannot replicate the lifestyle we had together. Most women's lives are going to be financially compromised after divorce.

You have to become knowledgeable about how much money you have coming in, how much you can spend on housing and all the necessities of life and still live in liquidity. In other words, what can you afford that allows you to also have some cash on hand. The rule of thumb I use is 60 percent of after-tax income goes to all living expenses, 20 percent is discretionary, and 20 percent should go into savings or an investment or retirement fund.

That means you might end up in a two-bedroom apartment, and that's okay. You may have to move. I moved from Manhattan to Philadelphia and I love it. I'm still in a great city and I can get to New York in an hour if I want to. Everything is much less expensive here, including housing, compared to New York. You can get your needs met and live in an environment you want by making modifications to your living situation.

WHAT ABOUT PLANNING FOR THE FUTURE, ESPECIALLY FOR WOMEN WHO MAY HAVE BEEN DEPENDING ON THEIR HUSBAND'S RETIREMENT INCOME FOR THEIR OWN RETIREMENT?

Understand your retirement goals. Talk to a financial planner. Check out a retirement calculator online and get ready to be shocked. Often times these tools tell you that between two and three million dollars are necessary to take care of your retirement. That means if you have not saved and you are in your forties or fifties you need to put away between one thousand and two thousand a month, maybe more, to meet that goal. That sends many women into a money coma. Don't do that. Get in alignment with your goals; you don't want to have nothing. Start somewhere; even if you can get close to one million through saving and investing, that's better than nothing.

HOW ELSE CAN WOMEN PREPARE FOR RETIREMENT?

Stop thinking about it as a finite point in time. Retirement is a made-up concept. We packaged it in this country as something that happens when you turn sixty-five. But that's not realistic. Very few people can afford to stop working at sixty-five, and many don't want to. First and foremost, have a marketable skill. If you don't have one, learn one. I know computer programming, and I make sure I write code at my job to keep my chops up and to stay on top of new information. I don't have to be a programmer right now, but someday I might have to go back to it and I want to be ready. Web skills aren't that difficult to learn, and you can make fifty or seventy-five dollars an hour at them, if you're good. I recommend skillcrush.com as an affordable way to learn technical skills. And it's geared toward women.

Of course you have to learn how to hustle to get clients. Selling services can be intimidating and there is so much rejection. A lot of people don't realize three no's on first ask is normal. There can be many more no's before you get a yes. Learning what it means to build a sales pipeline is another skill you need in order to make your primary skill profitable.

WHAT ELSE CAN THE NEW SINGLE DO TO IMPROVE HER POSTDIVORCE LIFE?

I see working moms with young children who feel isolated and exasperated. We do not help each other and it is not sustainable.

How do we reinvent village life? Young moms need help, older women need help with living situations. We have to find a way to create a community. We all thought we were supposed to do everything on our own and we can't. We all have to start helping each other more. Let's find someone in our community and help her, and tell her how she could help us. The idea of mutual co-operation is really the only sustainable way we can live.

Dating, Debt, and Don't Do It

While finances and money are always tied into divorce, realize that once you move into a new and exciting relationship you will want to start to forget what you went through in the last one. A friend of mine started dating what she called "a great guy." He was funny, smart, sweet, and creative. He had two children, an ex-wife, a dog, and a LOT OF DEBT. They dated for a little while and she always wound up with the check, especially after elaborate dinners at fine restaurants that he had suggested. This pattern went on for months and it made her feel used—and it made her poor.

She was not upset by the fact that she made more money than he did, but she was upset that it was she, and *only* she, who was forking over her hard-earned money so they could have a great time. In the end, she was honest with him by telling him that she, too, was recently out of a divorce and didn't have the extra money to support his dating place habits. Unfortunately, without her generous supply of cash, he eventually moved on. She was sad about it, but the sadness was short-lived and tempered by gratitude that she had cut her losses before she was so deeply tied to him that she could not distinguish why he was with her.

When I was at my most miserable—just before and just

after—my divorce, work saved me. Since a big chunk of my time was spent on-air, I literally could not afford to let myself go: I had to maintain my weight, my grooming, and my style in order to look qualified and professional on camera. The particulars of my job also meant I met interesting people and learned about new and interesting things and ideas. The more I threw myself into my work, the more absorbed by it I became, and the less time I had for moping or grinding my teeth in anger.

I am aware of the rare privilege I have in this arena of my life. I love my job and am thankful for it every day. I hope you share this circumstance with me, but if you do not, my advice is to pretend, just for a little while, that you do. Work, even the mundane kind, gives you: income; a place to go to get out of the house or apartment; self-satisfaction and independence; and colleagueship. Most important, work gives you continuity and stability at a time in your life when you most need them.

Chart Your Course

As you chart your life as a New Single, you may begin to think about other changes that would make you happy, and on that list might be a new career, or a new setting for the work you currently do. Now is the time for research and planning—don't make the mistake my friend made by assuming that because she could shop she could sell and dive right into a new endeavor without first testing the waters.

You'd be amazed at the educational opportunities available for retraining to begin a second career, if that is your interest. Many are online, and many more are close by at a community college and can be completed in the short term, anywhere from six months to two years. There are weekend degree programs that offer MBAs and other applied (and remunerative) advanced degrees.

If you are entering the workforce after a long hiatus, you might want to check with your local library for résumé-writing workshops, employment support groups, and job-hunting resources. Don't hesitate to let your friends know you are looking for work. It may take time—scratch that, it *will* take time—to get back into the swing of nine to five or seven to midnight, but a new job will become part of the identity you are crafting as a New Single.

A-TEAM FEATURE

Own Your Talents

Jen Groover is a serial entrepreneur, author, motivational speaker, and host of PBS's *Empowered*. She spoke to me about career and how to make sure yours is on a rising track.

IF A WOMAN HAS ALLOWED HER CAREER TO LAG OR BECOME DERAILED, HOW CAN SHE GET BACK ON TRACK? WHAT ARE SOME OF THE FIRST STEPS SHE SHOULD TAKE?

Getting your career back on track is a core part of getting yourself back on track. See this step as getting a part of you back. Reflect on who you are, why you do what you do, or why you would want to do something differently. What type of impact do you want to make? What are you passionate about? What's your purpose?

I don't believe in the mind-set that we are supposed to do something we hate for the rest of our lives just to make money. I believe this is damaging to your soul and is emotionally draining. After going through a divorce, or anything challenging, you should seek things that make your soul come alive. This is part of healing. Getting your career back on track, even if you choose a different path, is really about getting yourself on the path in life you were meant to be on, that is where you will truly thrive.

IF A WOMAN DID NOT WORK DURING HER MARRIAGE, WHAT ARE SOME TIPS ON GETTING BACK IN THE WORKFORCE?

If a woman took time off during her marriage to raise her family or explore other passions, to effectively enter back into the workforce she needs to communicate that decision as an empowered choice that she made for herself and family. If you walk into an employer and project that you are a victim then that will project weakness and lack of conviction of your own choices. Evaluate all of the experiences you had during that time period, along with all of the skill sets you gained, even if they seem nontraditional, and explore how they can be "marketed" as transferable experiences to whatever career path you are seeking.

HOW DO YOU CREATE A WINNING RÉSUMÉ, ESPECIALLY IF YOU HAVE NOT WORKED IN A WHILE, OR IF YOUR CAREER WAS STALLED DURING YOUR RELATIONSHIP?

The digital age has really changed the ways a résumé can pop. As an entrepreneur, we don't use résumés, we send "bios" out and digital presentations, press kits, or videos. I would encourage you to shift from a résumé mind-set to a digital presentation mind-set. Aesthetics really do matter, so you can make a digital portfolio with images that tell stories, too. Social media has not only advanced people's acceptance of this, but have almost made it a necessity for reviewers to stay engaged.

In your presentation, include life experiences and how they translate to knowledge and skill sets. Perhaps even volunteer/intern at places to gain experiences quickly, which also shows taking initiative to learn. If you have volunteered, don't forget to use those experiences as an opportunity to get referrals/testimonials about your work ethic and the value you added to the experience.

Also remember, you are "selling" the value you can add to an environment. Your "résumé" needs to convey passion, enthusiasm, charisma, and all of the other qualities that make people want to be around others in any environment. It's not just about past accomplishments any longer, most employers consider your potential for the future. As an employer, I would always take someone who is passionate, ambitious, willing to learn, and emotionally intelligent over someone who lacks those things but came from a great school and worked at great places. Confidence and belief in your worth are always key.

Being in Balance

Whether you are a diehard career woman, a stay-at-home mom, or just trying to do it all, the emotional aftermath can take its toll, but it doesn't have to take your balance. In fact, working hard to separate your money and your career from your emotions will allow you to make the right decisions about what to do next.

CHAPTER NINE

We Are Family and Friends

*"Life is like riding a bicycle. To keep your
balance, you must keep moving."*

—ALBERT EINSTEIN

When we are rebooting our lives and starting over, we are certainly not doing it alone, whether we're part of a large family or maintain a close-knit group of friends. In either case, there is no question that your relationships within your family and your circle of friends will change. The people in those groups will change. Some family members (the ones who couldn't stand your ex) will embrace you with new fervor. Some friends, let's face it, will drop you like a hot potato. This group is typically made up of married friends with whom you and your ex went to dinner with, or took in plays together, or just spent time with. The "new you" does not belong in this picture anymore. Make no mistake, you will be erased from it. This chapter addresses the new relationships you will form, and the old ones you will maintain. I'd pay special attention to sticky situations you might find yourself in. I know I did!

Cherish the Handful

First, though, the good news: The "old" friends you do keep are the best. My mother, who was my very best friend until her too-soon death from breast cancer in 1990, taught me early on that true friendship is a rare and precious commodity. You can have lots of pals, people you hang out with and have good times with, she said, but you will probably be able to count the number of friends you have on the fingers of one hand.

My mother said if you have a handful of friends, good friends and real friends, your life is golden. I am talking about the friends who remind you what is important in life and the kind who make all the tears feel silly after a conversation with them. As I have gone through life, people have come and gone in and out of it, but I have learned to cherish the handful of friends who help when the chips are down and never, ever turned their backs on me, despite the fact that I felt I failed them when I failed what I thought was a fairy-tale marriage.

I understand now what my mother was telling me: it is not the quantity of the people in your life; it is the quality and depth of your bond with them and theirs with you. When you find these forever friends, make sure they know they are cherished. Having a strong circle of friends is important during and after a time like this; here's a quick look at how to really access the people around you.

Do your friends build you up and give you strength? Do you feel like you could do anything after a conversation with them? My best friend, Diane Danois, is someone I cherish every day. We talk in the morning before she goes to work. Even though she got married several years ago, we have always maintained a very close friendship and I never felt like a third wheel around her and her husband. She listened to me repeat one story after another during my separation and my divorce and now my dating life. We have love and respect for each other's lives and I feel like she is family. Make sure your closest friends do the same for you and you for them.

Do your friends encourage you to aspire to do more in life? Are they proud of your accomplishments or do they compete with you every time you tell them something you have done? Make sure the people you are around are not competing with you and making you feel anything less than whole.

Do you feel like an open book with your friends or do you hide things to avoid hearing their opinion because they always feel they know what is best for you? At one point in my life I felt like I needed to be talking to someone 24/7 to avoid having to give my current situation any real thought. I would literally search for a few people to call consistently. I remember that one person who was always strong never had a shortage of opinions for me. In time, though, I realized she would get insulted if I didn't take her advice without questioning it or if I tried to use her advice to form my own conclusions. It was time for us to say goodbye. She had been a great friend to me for many years and I to her, but when I started to dread hearing her responses or getting a phone call, I realized it was not fair to either of us to continue a friendship like that.

I began to hate myself a little bit because I realized I had been using her as a receptacle for dumping my angst. When she demanded to have her ego stroked in return by my blind acceptance of her counsel, I just couldn't do it. This kind of one-sided friendship—I took from her but gave her nothing in return—is always doomed. Better to cool its intensity so that you can remain on cordial terms and occasionally still enjoy each other's company.

THAT'S GRATITUDE FOR YOU

I can think of two little words that you're probably not saying often enough right now. Two little words that might just change your life: thank you. The thing is, up to this point, and for many points moving forward, you have needed and you will continue to need your friends. They made a conscious effort to help you through your time of crisis; it's up to you to let them know how much you appreciate it. So, say thank you.

But how? How you express your gratitude has a lot to do with how far your BFFs went for you. If they were talking you off a ledge or chasing you with a butterfly net, then you might want to do a little more than stop at the Hallmark store. In any case, they've been an ear for your problems and a shoulder to cry on. They went the extra mile for you. Now, go the extra mile for them.

Here are five ways to let your friends know you appreciate them.

1. Spend time together, talking about them. You don't have to even let them know you are doing it. But a simple cup of coffee along with your time is more than any expensive gift you can give.

2. Offer to help them with watching their dog, or child care for a day or a night so they are freed up to do what they want. In this world we are so busy with ourselves, we forget how good it feels to help someone else.

3. Be different. It's easy to send cards or a cookie bouquet—but be a little original. I love to send macaroons from this amazing shop in the West Village. People don't usually spend money like that on themselves and it is seldom forgotten.

4. Remember the little things people say. My friend Diane, who helped me through my divorce, loved this chocolate store in London—I happened to be there in the throes of my divorce and went by and sent her a surprise of chocolate from London. It wasn't her birthday or anniversary, it was just me saying I remember you and love you like you have loved me.

5. Dinner's on you. But don't be cliché. One night I invited three of my dearest friends to my house to say thank you. I made a huge pot of pasta, the wine was flowing and I set up a cheese table with all sorts of cheeses on it to choose from (my sister-in-law's idea). We played a board game and told stories and had a blast. To this day, it's the night everyone talks about. It was special and it was all about them.

By the way, saying thank you actually makes you happier, too. According to a study by the John Templeton Foundation, 64 percent of women say they say thank you simply because it makes them feel good. And other researchers say saying thank you decreases stress.

How to Handle Those Sticky Situations

Sticky Situation 1: Family Gatherings and Holidays

In the best of all possible worlds, you love your family, and better yet, you actually like the individuals who collectively make up this oddball assortment of characters who share your DNA. If this is the case, then family gatherings should be a breeze.

Even so, if you absolutely dread showing up at Uncle Howie's seventy-fifth birthday bash alone, then don't—and by that I mean don't miss the party, just don't show up alone. It's a *family* gathering, remember? Call your sister or your cousin or your niece and make arrangements to go with them. You'll have support when you need it most—crossing the threshold for the first time as a New Single, and—if you're really smart—a "time-to-go" signal arranged for when you've had enough familial conviviality.

Holidays, though, can be more unsettling. The key to getting through them, and maybe even enjoying them, is to face up to the fact that things have changed. Do not even try to keep things "just the same." They are not, and pretending otherwise does more harm than good. You'll be miserable—and if you have kids, and if you have custody of them for a holiday, they will be miserable, too, if everything is the same as it always was, except Daddy's not around to carve the turkey or take the gang out for ice cream.

Your first holiday as a New Single is the hardest. This advice is cliché because it is true. There are several strategies you can use, however, to lessen the pain.

LESSONS FROM SMART WOMEN

"You can survive without living by someone else's choices! For me it has been pure freedom. I raised my daughter with sole custody and sole support, she always chose when she wanted to see her father while growing up. My daughter is now an independent, intelligent, and compassionate human being. She thrived and is studying to be a psychologist!

> Divorce is the beginning of a new chapter in your life and you can make it a positive change. Be strong and your friends and family will embrace you!'
> —Helen Powers, legendary fit model for thirty years and lifestyle advocate, www.helenpowers.com

Strategy One: Spend the holiday alone

I know it's counterintuitive, but for some of us a quiet Christmas, curled up with a book, some hot chocolate, and a cozy afghan is medicine for the soul. Maybe you go to your best friend's home for cocktails on Christmas Eve, or have a Boxing Day brunch with your cousins. Either way, you have some holiday cheer, but you also have given yourself the space to just get through it. There—you've done it, and by the time the holiday comes around again you will have established your new life and will be able to create new traditions. Give yourself the gift of time.

Strategy Two: Get out of town

A change of scenery can be incredibly healing for the holiday blues you fear during the first round of special days you spend as an ex. When was the last time you went home for Thanksgiving? A quick visit to an out-of-town relative or friend will remind you of the folks whose continuing presence in your life you can remain grateful for. Everybody loves to set an extra place at the holiday table; trust me—you will be welcomed with open arms.

Not feeling in the mood for company? You still might want to get out of town. There are incredible deals to be had in the finest hotels in cities across the US and abroad around Christmas. You can pamper yourself silly in sybaritic luxury for a fraction of the cost at a different time of year. One friend of mine told me about her sister, a fifty-something single, who every year books herself into the Gold Floor of Boston's Copley Plaza for three nights between Christmas and New Year's. She takes advantage of the Gold Floor perks—especially the library and parlors, which re-create a Boston town house, complete with crackling fire—and strolls the shops on Boylston and Newbury streets, taking in the decorated windows. At night she has no problem securing a great table at one of Boston's top restaurants, and for those few days and nights she lives the life of a Proper Bostonian.

Another friend of a friend, Bobbie, traveled by air on Christmas Day to go skiing in Vermont with her teenage son. The airport was empty, security was speedy, and there was plenty of room to spread out on the plane. Bobbie and her kid spent their days on the slopes and their nights playing Scrabble. When they returned home, each felt the exercise and the brisk New England air had drained away the tension and anxiety each had felt on the run-up to the holiday.

You may not be in a financial position to take a holiday break, but you *can* afford a "staycation" wherein you act like a tourist in your own town—visit a gallery or a historic house in holiday dress. You might even consider volunteering a few hours for charity or for friends who also need a break. If you long to see the holiday through the eyes of a child, arrange to look after a friend's child or children for an afternoon. A matinee of *The*

Nutcracker, perhaps? An afternoon at the roller rink? Your friend will thank you, and you'll feel great.

Strategy Three: Accept what you cannot change

You are dreading the Fourth of July weekend. Your ex has the kids and he's taking them to Washington, DC, for the capitol concert and fireworks. As a two-parent family, the summer holiday was one you treasured, and the kids really looked forward to the patriotic hoopla. Without your family, the last thing you feel like is a firecracker. Is there anything you can do to *not* feel miserable? Frankly, no, there is not. The family you are missing does not exist anymore. You and your ex changed all that when you got divorced. The rituals of family life pertaining to holidays and vacations are now governed by the terms of your divorce decree. If he has the kids over Labor Day, that's just the way it is and the way it is going to be unless those terms change. All you can, and *should,* do is everything in your power to make sure your children have the best possible time they can.

That means no visible resentment of their plans with their father, no teary prolonged goodbyes. You might very well feel miserable when you hand over your daughter to her father for the first time after your divorce. He'll probably feel miserable, too, when he hands her back. You still have that much in common, at least. This is the time for you to remember that you are a grown-up, even if you feel like a lost child. Suck it up and be strong for your kids. Going forward, do the best you can to put your children's welfare and well-being first when it comes to dealing with your ex in front of them.

Sticky Situation 2: No Kidding

The phone rang during a commercial break. Vibrated, actually.

"Are you sitting?" A PR friend of mine was on the other end.

"Are you kidding me? I'm about to go on the air."

"That interview you did about waiting to have kids. Yeah, the story they pitched wasn't exactly the story they went with." The *New York Post* asked to talk to me for a story about career-focused women who had decided to wait a few years before entering parenthood. I agreed to be interviewed and talked about how I had wanted children when I was married, but since I was single again I realized that being childless, at least for now, was actually a good thing.

When the "interview" appeared in the paper, there I was, in a full-page photo with another woman and the headline: WE SAY NO TO BABIES AND YES TO NYC. The O in "NO" was a screaming baby with a red line through it. And the Y in "YES" was a martini glass. I looked and sounded like I was some baby-hating, booze hound monster. I was mortified. Again.

I do not regret that my ex-husband and I did not have a child while we were married, and now that we are not, I am rather glad we did not. This is not to say that I don't want children in the future. I do. I want to raise my child in a loving and stable household. Until then, I will baby my adorable nephew and make goo-goo eyes at my friend's kids.

Sticky Situation 3: I Love My Kids, But Can I Please Have a Date?

Actress Idina Menzel doesn't mince words when it comes to describing what it's like to be a single mother who's ready to put herself back into circulation. While writing this book, I heard a radio interview with Menzel, who said, "It all sucks," referring to her split with Taye Diggs, ex-hubby and the father of her son. She was talking about dating as a single mom and her breakup and the difficulty of introducing her son to men she is trying to date.

I'll let you in on a little secret, if you promise to keep it to yourself. Most single or divorced men over the age of forty actually seem to *prefer* to date and enter into relationships with a divorced woman, rather than one who's never been married. So right there you have a big edge over the competition. The fact that you have children will bother you more than it will him— and with good reason, they're *your* kids! You *should* be concerned about them!

The point is: having children does not mean you must stay at home with them until they leave for college. It does mean that you must plan your social life to blend in as seamlessly as possible into their established routines. Timing your dates to coincide with when your ex has the kids is the obvious place to start. Lunch dates can be scheduled when the children are in school.

Should your new relationship reach the point at which you want to introduce your beau to your child, trust your instincts. You know your child better than anybody else, so think about what will feel the most natural for her: inviting your friend to a home-cooked dinner with just the three of you? Meeting up to walk the dogs then have ice cream in the park? Remember that your child *is* a child, which means her world revolves around her. She might be uneasy about "sharing" you. She might be confused about who this stranger is. Encourage her to talk to you and express her worries. Reassure her that she'll always be your daughter and you'll always be her mom—and that both of you will always share your journey through life. Meeting others along the way is part of the journey for you and her.

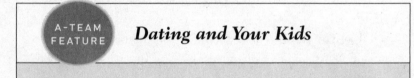

Dating and Your Kids

A-TEAM FEATURE

Kerri Zane is an internationally recognized single-mom lifestyle expert, coparenting authority, speaker, spokesperson, and Emmy award–winning television executive producer. She is also the Amazon best-selling author of *It Takes All 5: A Single Mom's Guide to Finding the REAL One*. Kerri has an MA in spiritual psychology from the University of Santa Monica and a BA from UCLA. A divorced single mom, Kerri lives in Long Beach, California, with her two daughters and two Siamese cats. Here she gives us the 4-1-1 on dating when you have kids.

HOW MUCH INFORMATION DO YOU WANT TO SHARE WITH YOUR CHILDREN?

How much and what you share with your children depends on their age. But don't be fooled, kids are very astute; they know when you are going out on a date vs. hanging with family or your girlfriends. You dress differently. You never want to role-model lying to your children, so tell them the truth. If your kids are younger it is sufficient to say that you are going out for some adult time, without sharing specifics. As long as they feel secure with their babysitter and know they can reach you via cell phone if there is an emergency you should be good to go.

If your kids are middle schoolers or older, it's okay to tell them that you are going out on a date. Teens are most likely dating themselves and get that you need connections with people your age. No matter how old children are, eight or thirty-eight, you need to reassure them with your unconditional love. Let them know in no uncertain terms that NO ONE is replacing them. They will always be first in your heart.

SHOULD SINGLE PARENTS LOOK TO DATE PEOPLE WHO ALREADY HAVE CHILDREN?

Dating people who also have children does have its benefits. You both understand the machinations of juggling schedules. But, I wouldn't absolutely preclude dating those who don't have kids. In either case be clear that, for better or worse, kids will take priority.

IS THERE A RIGHT TIME TO INTRODUCE YOUR KIDS TO YOUR BOYFRIEND?

Yes. My rule of thumb is three to six months. You don't want to do it too soon in case the relationship doesn't work out. If kids get too attached and you as a couple don't work it could potentially be tantamount to another breakup for them. If you wait too long it's not good either. They will feel like you've been hiding him from them.

What is the best way to introduce your children to someone you are dating?

Again, a lot depends on their age. Overall, I would not recommend you take your new significant other to your kid's school or sports activities. Your children want the focus to be on them, not the new guy. You may also not want the new guy around the ex. It can be awkward and uncomfortable. My suggestion is to choose a neutral place, for a brief twenty- to thirty-minute visit, doing something that you know your kids will enjoy, like an ice cream date.

What single parent dating sites do you recommend?

For the over-forty women and single moms I prefer AYI.com. It offers all the benefits of a large dating pool site and has complete integration with Facebook, which gives singles the friends-of-friends litmus test, as well as iOS and Android applications to make dating on the go easy. For people who are very targeted in their interests and want to meet someone like-minded, the Warehouse Dating Group has over thirteen hundred dating sites to explore. They maintain sites like Trek Dating, for *Star Trek* fans, to gay-single-parent dating, Date Gingers, and the more general Singles Warehouse.

Should I wait until my kids are grown to date?

No. That kind of thinking is unhealthy for you and your children. Current research indicates that an unhealthy social life is as bad as (or worse than) being an alcoholic, smoking fifteen cigarettes a day, or being obese. It adds to your stress level. So me time is as important as eating right and exercising. Also, it's important to note that when you have a social life separate from your children it's not only good role modeling but it also takes the pressure off of them to feel the need to entertain you. Everyone gets to "play" with friends their own age.

HOW DO YOU DIVIDE QUALITY TIME BETWEEN MOTHERHOOD AND DATING?

There is no doubt about the fact that single motherhood is a masterful juggling act. In my experience, the best way to divide quality time is to compartmentalize. Go to that place of truly being present to what is going on in that moment. When you are with your children be very focused on them and their needs. When you are at work be laser-beam focused on the task at hand.

WHO DO YOU ASK FOR HELP?

A common guilt trap for single moms is the belief that they can (and should) be omnipresent. It's impossible, unnecessary, and exhausting. Being able to delegate child care duties is a gift. My advice to women just starting the divorce process is to consider how you can create a custody arrangement that allows for you to spend time with your children and time for yourself. As much as you might not like your ex, your kids do, and they need their Daddy time. Think of him as your trusted built-in babysitter. Your noncustodial time is the perfect opportunity to schedule personal downtime and dating escapades or to do the work or house projects you need to get done. If that doesn't work for you, Dad is just out of the picture, or your former spouse is physically or emotionally abusive or unfit to be a parent because of drugs or alcohol then you're going to want to engage the almighty "village."

Here are some options:

- Offer to tag-team time-share with other single moms. This can work well for both moms, as children often would rather play with their peers than adults. Where do you find other single moms? At your kids' school, meetup.com, mommeetmom.com.

- Consider an after-school mother's helper. These are older children in the neighborhood, usually around eleven or twelve, who will play with your children and keep them occupied or be in the house in the event your child wakes from his/her nap.

- Enlist family and friends or consider a full-time caretaker. If you cannot afford that kind of help ask to buddy up with some of the other moms' helpers and give them a bit of extra money to cover your kids.

- Many communities and religious centers have child-care centers.

- Preteens and teen children are much more independent and can spend an hour or two by themselves. Get your kids involved in after-school activities and/or sports programs.

- Have a ready list of prospective neighborhood babysitters on your smart phone. There are lots of places on-

line to search for reliable and recommended sitters.
Check out babysitterbarter.com.

Bottom line: what is most important is not being afraid to ask
for what you need. Be open to accept the way other people do
things, show your appreciation for their efforts, and take the time
to enjoy your life.

HOW DO YOU EXPLAIN TO YOUR CHILD WHEN YOU OR YOUR EX BECOMES INVOLVED WITH ANOTHER PERSON?

Just as you've explained to your children about your dating, so
it goes for your ex. Even though your relationship did not work
out, you both still need to have adult companionship to do the
things that your kids can't or won't want to do with you or with
him.

HOW DO YOU MAKE SURE YOUR CHILD DOESN'T PICK UP ON YOUR ANGER TOWARD YOUR EX?

This is a critically important exercise in self-censuring. It's important to never lose sight of the fact that your ex is and will always be your kids' father. They want to love him and be loved by
him. Any expressed anger could backfire on you. Feel comforted
by the fact that people never change and whatever it is about your
former spouse that you found challenging may also become an
obstacle for your kids as they grow up and become more aware.
You will have your "told you so" day, without ever having to say it!

Sticky Situation 4: Be Ready for These Eight Words

"Let me know if you need a plus one." Those are the words that were glaring up at me from my phone one evening when the director of a new TV series invited me to a viewing party. It would not be the first time I had seen them, and as I knew in advance, it would not be the last.

I didn't exactly have a plus one at the time. I felt like a minus one more often than not. So, I scoured my brain trying to think of someone to take with me. It was a Friday night and most of my girlfriends had plans. Most of my boyfriends did, too. So, it was just me: party of one. Not party of one plus one.

I took me about an hour to press my respond "No, it will just be me."

His answer: "k."

With that, I decided that this was not going to be the last time I arrived at an event with my purse on my arm and nothing else. So, I made a plan. I decided to map out the night and it turns out instead of sitting there talking to no one, I worked the room and found everyone. Now I don't dread not having a plus one—I embrace it. And here is what I did to make sure I was prepared for any uncomfortable moments.

I arrived and found the host immediately and told him, "If you know anyone here I should know, can you introduce me and I'll take it from there." He did. And then I did. I spoke with a group that he introduced me to for a while, and then I went to the bar. I talked to the bartender, and made sure to smile at everyone who looked my way. By the end of the night, I forgot I was alone. But what I didn't forget was how confident I felt walking out of there and not wanting to cry. I didn't feel like I had no one, I felt like I was finally beginning to be someone again—and that someone wasn't just a party of one.

Sticky Situation 5: To Friend or to De-friend

When I use the word "friend" here, I use it lightly. If you are like so many of us, you had those "couple friends" or friends that you were friends with because he was friends with them. Are you still with me? The hope that we all have is people will be grown up and understanding that despite the fact that the two of you have "uncoupled," it's okay to continue to be friends with just half of the couple—or you as a person. Unfortunately, that is not always the case. If you find that some of the "friends" you had as a couple are no longer comfortable with you as a single— MOVE ON.

In fact, move on faster than you are doing with your ex. I had very little tolerance for people who did not see me as an individual both in and out of my marriage. I bring this up because I was recently talking to a former coworker who went through a divorce after nine years of marriage. She and her husband were friends with a number of couples in their neighborhood in Philadelphia. But, once they decided to split (and they are actually on good terms), a woman she was friends with was no longer comfortable speaking with her. She didn't return phone calls, never called to see how my friend was doing, and was truly uncomfortable with the fact that my friend was no longer part of a couple.

No matter the reason, you don't have time to figure out

fair-weather friends. Please, I know it's not easy, but try to accept this and move forward. It will bring you to a better place with better people. You don't need to find a way to put yourself in the path of rejection or of someone who is only there because of circumstance and not because she truly wants to be with you.

A-TEAM FEATURE   *Time for a Transition*

Friends and family are what help us with the challenges we face. And, of course, during a time of transition, they are more important than ever. This is a transition for a lot of people in a lot of ways. Perhaps you are going through a breakup early in life, but a majority of divorces happen when women are nearing or have reached their forties. I called my dear friend Judy Goss, founder and CEO of Over 40 Females (www.over40females.com). She is a former model, but beautiful both on the outside and the inside. Her goal was to give women a platform to be heard and to encourage them to network and connect as they transition in life. Here's what she had to say.

HOW DO FRIENDS AND FAMILY INSPIRE US AS WE ARE GOING THROUGH A TRANSITION IN LIFE?

They give us hope, energy, and love, which is important for your spiritual side. If you let them, friends can lift the pressure you feel when transitioning with a positive word or sound advice, and family can alleviate your stress by loving you unconditionally. It is important to have a balance of work and a strong spiritual side to stay focused, positive, and ready for anything. Your spiritual side will give you strength and let you be loved by your friends and family!

What is the number one secret to transitioning into another part of your life whether it's your breakup or your age?

You need to keep moving forward—NO MATTER WHAT. I have been through divorce, layoffs, bankruptcy, miscarriages—sometimes all at once!—and the key is to keep taking a step forward no matter how small or insignificant you think that step is. Going through transitions, especially at an older age, can be intimidating and scary. You need to keep your head up and look toward the future instead of concentrating on looking behind you and what the past has brought you. Take that step to better yourself each day, and before you know it the steps will get bigger and bigger and transform into your ultimate success.

What is the biggest challenge women who are approaching forty or are over forty face?

Stamina. We surveyed women over forty about this, and it is a huge issue. Suddenly, it is harder to work so many hours, stay up late, or just workout regularly. Especially since more women are having kids later in life—it can be tough! We must take the initiative and keep up with our health, take vitamins, and figure out how we can have more energy.

ADVICE FOR A WOMAN WHO HAS DECIDED TO START OVER AGAIN WHEN IT COMES TO HER CAREER OR A NEW CAREER?

Learn everything you can about your new career before you switch! If you are an entrepreneur, what are the sales potentials? How are you going to market yourself/product/service? Do you have the budget/time to invest in a new idea? And if you are going to work for a corporation, what is the background of the company? Can you speak to someone who works there and find out what the environment is like? Do they offer incentives? The best way to make a change is to research, test your market, and talk to others who either work the same career or have made a similar change.

The New Single on the Job

I have found that job hunting and success in the workplace are a lot like dating. There are ways to do it well and then there are things that you never want to repeat again! I put together a few things to keep in mind whether you are looking to start a new career or a new job following your breakup or if you have one and you are working hard to move ahead.

Be Positive

It is definitely easier said than done. And at a time like this, the last thing you want to do is be a Debbie Downer, not only for yourself, but for the people around you. Every time I swipe my card to go into work I say a little thank you to the universe for allowing me to be there. Yes, we all have days that are stressful and exhausting. And I am often ready for the weekend before Wednesday hits, but at the end of the day, I am grateful for what I have been given and I always try to remember to appreciate it. Even if you are in the middle of a job search, say thank you every step of the way.

Keep Learning

This is critical. The world is changing at an alarming yet exciting rate. But it is not chic to say, "I'm not a tech person," or "I hate social media." That is well and good, but if you are looking to stay young in the world, you are going to have to keep learning. It doesn't have to cost you a penny, but it is worth every second of your time to do it. Take Apple classes, talk to your kids, your nephew, or your niece about the newest, latest, and greatest apps or Web site out there, and take the time to just learn on your own. It is not enough to know just the basics anymore. My seventy-five-year-old father kept up with the times and is now just as tech savvy as my brother. It was not because it came easy to him, but because it was essential.

Just Say Yes

I have said this a few times now, but you must say yes. This time, though, I am not talking about dating, instead I am talking about networking. You never know who you are going to meet along the way. Take your cards and your smile and make sure you just show up when you are invited to network at an industry function or dinner party and sell yourself. It doesn't matter if you are perfectly happy in the job, you should always know what is out there and always be a step ahead.

Invest in Yourself Without Apology

This can be a tough one to hear, but I learned over time it is the one approach that truly works. If you want to make money, sometimes in business you have to spend money or at least invest in the basics to get ahead. I learned this one the hard way—when you are cheap in this area and you don't have the proper tools you need for yourself, your career, or your corporation—it can hurt you in the end. You don't have to have the most expensive of anything, but you do need to be in the game. So, if you need a laptop, a tablet, an iPhone, the right clothes, or the right car to be better at your job—please invest in PROJECT YOU first.

You Want It? Ask for It

I remember for so many years I would complain that I wasn't making enough money or I wasn't far enough in my career. But, the problem was that while I was sitting there complaining about it—someone else was asking for it.

No one is going to do it for you. If you want something, you have to ask for it. No exceptions. If you want a raise, don't make a big deal out of it. Write down the reasons, make an appointment with your boss, and then ask for it.

If you want a new position or a new job, don't bemoan the

fact you don't have it, write down the steps to getting it and go after it. The sticky notes on my Mac have been a lifesaver for me. I have tons of them and they are always filled up with my lists and my plans and my dreams. Write down your dreams. See them. And then, make them happen.

CHAPTER TEN

The New Single in a New Relationship—The Last Ninety Days and Beyond

"Do one thing every day that scares you."

—Mary Schmich

Right around the time my divorce was finalized, a doctor whom I had met at a party invited me to dinner. Since he was generally considered "a catch," I agreed, even though I was nowhere near ready for any kind of serious relationship. Just a date, I thought. He had made a reservation at a trendy place close to my office after making sure there were plenty of vegetarian items on the menu. He's considerate, I thought—good sign.

We did the usual hellos as I sat down at the table. It was one of those half-circle booths so you have no choice but to sit next to the person and then try to talk to him while looking at him from the side because it is so awkward, especially on a first date.

As we made our way from the menu to the first topic, I noticed he was staring at me from the corners of my mouth, back up to my eyes, back down to my mouth. I asked, "Is everything okay?" I was worried I was wearing food on my face, so I touched my face with my napkin to make sure. As a doctor, his specialty was dermatology, so his scrutiny took on an almost clinical feeling.

He answered my question with one of his own: "How old are you? I Googled you—it said forty-three."

I was a little shocked, but thanks to the Internet, a girl no longer has the luxury of keeping her age to herself. "Yes, I'm forty-three," I answered.

"Well, you look like you have good genes. Do you want kids? I think we could have good heat."

Yep. "I think we could have good heat." Seven words that are burned into my dating diary forever. Words that went from haunting to humiliating to eventually hilarious. The fact that I was coming off of a public divorce, dealing with giving up part of my business, and trying to remain put-together, it seemed like the good doctor was putting a lot on my plate before the main course was served. Nevertheless, I answered him. "To be honest," I said, "I did want children at one point in my life. But, as you know the best-laid plans—"

"Well, I spent the last two decades building my practice," he replied. "I have a sixteen-year-old daughter from my first wife. I wouldn't mind having another child—you have good genes."

I tell you this story because it was one of many shocking conversations that came on rather fast. The one thing I was definitely not ready for were intimate conversations with complete strangers. But one date after another, I sat wondering why men felt so free to bring up personal things with me that I had not even spoken to myself about.

My story is not unique. In fact, it's quite the opposite. I never intended to be writing a book called *The New Single*. In fact, after I said, "I do," I never intended to be single again. But, as much as I worked to predict, plan, and proceed to my future, little did I know my path was destined to go in a direction I was not prepared for. I was especially not prepared for the questions my dates would ask.

Be Prepared: Tamsen's Top Awkward Questions

QUESTION: WHOSE FAULT WAS IT?

My answer: No one's. No matter how it played out in the press, my former husband and I were in a relationship and it didn't work out. But to turn and cast blame on either of the parties is not only unfair, quite frankly it's a waste of time.

QUESTION: COULD YOU HAVE WORKED IT OUT?

This question always shocked me, though I now have an answer for it: Yes. It could have worked out. We would have been two people living separate and lonely lives just to be able to live together.

I didn't come to the conclusion to divorce quickly. In fact, I fought it for as long as I could. To this day, there are things I would never talk about out of respect for the relationship that once was something very special. I know it's not easy, especially when there are a lot of emotions involved or if you are the party who still wants to see things work out. Remember that the details of your breakup are no one's business but yours and your ex's. Keep it that way.

Be prepared with a short answer: no, and a quick change

of subject. Alternatively—this works best if you are in a very public space with lots of people you know around—burst into tears, shriek invective at your date, and yell that meddlesome questions like his are the reason things didn't work out. You won't be asked that question again any time soon by anyone within earshot. Trust me. You also probably won't be asked out on a second date.

QUESTION: Do you still want kids?

First comes love. Then comes marriage. Then comes (insert name) in the baby carriage. That little rhyme never told us what to do in case we have to insert a divorce into the line between the marriage and the carriage. Being a single woman without children from my first marriage, I tackle this question a lot. And people are not afraid to ask me this one head-on. Here is the truth: it's none of their business. Here is the other truth: they still ask and they still want an answer. I am always pretty candid. I would love to have a child. I don't. It hurt . . . a great deal. But, I am where I am supposed to be right now. That is the answer I give. If it is a man asking on a date, you should be honest. Don't pretend it's okay you don't when you secretly want children. This is your "new"—treat it as such. Start fresh. And be real.

QUESTION: Did you pick your career over your marriage?

If you are a woman with a job, get ready to answer this question repeatedly. It usually comes from someone who has been in a relationship for a long time or during a first date. Either way, it's an assumption people make because they are under the impression that if you are single or you are no longer in a relationship that somehow you decided your job was more important than your partner. I am sure there are some cases in which this happens. In fact, I am sure there are many cases in which this happens. Mine did not happen to be one of them. I simply have a job and had my relationship end. The two were in no way connected.

Instead of being insulted, irritated, or incredulous at this inquiry—chalk it up to the fact that people will be curious and not really understand what they are asking. I always classified this as more of an accusation than a question, but it is worth noting, it will come up at some point. Since my career saved me rather than destroyed my marriage, I used to find myself a bit defensive about this inquiry. Now, I simply assume that people are either curious or trying to tell me something, and despite the fact this is nobody's business—I tell them the truth: in no way did my career factor in my divorce. Easy. Simple. Over.

He Will Be Single. He Will Not Be "Sort of" Single

Yes, we are going there. Not because I want to, but because we have to. I am not sure why single women are attractive to certain married men. In fact, it perplexes me especially in this digital age, when every single character (literally and figuratively) is so easily Snapchat'd or What's App'd or Tweeted. Yes, I am making light of it, though it's anything but.

If you learn nothing else from this book—repeat after me: *I am no one's second choice.* Yes, even if he says he loves you and that he and his wife are still together only for the kids. Even if he says he is going to leave her but it's financial or even if he just wants a good time—please turn on your stilettos and run. A married man is not on the menu. In fact, to go one step further, I am going to list the lines that you may hear just so you don't think you have run into the married man who is the exception.

- We are not divorced because of the kids.

- We sleep in separate beds.

- I don't love her anymore. We are friends and really always have been.

- We are getting a divorce, but it's taking a long time due to how long we have been together.

- We are only together due to finances.

- We have an open relationship. We both see other people.

I am far from a prude, but I am trying to save you from a lot of heartache, downtime alone, and holidays spent being angry at someone who was never there for you to begin with. This brings me to the next subject: boundaries.

Be Aware You Need Boundaries

Dating again sounds simple enough. But the goal is not to find a guy to date. The goal is to date as the person you are now. I found myself falling back into old patterns when I first started back out on the singles scene. I was putting men into lists. I was making sure they fit into all the right categories. I was not being honest with myself as to what was really going to make me happy. When

I got married I was in my midthirties and thinking about a family and a long life together with my ex. Dating in my forties was a different story.

Getting Back Out There

1. Initially Have Fun. Don't Look for Love.

Bottom line, what you "need" is to have fun, not fall in love right now. After a breakup or a divorce, many people think, "I have to get out there and I need to fall in love again. I need to find a partner." That is not the case. It's critical to figure out who YOU are first. Figure out *what* you need. You don't need to have something just because someone else has it. Also, you don't "need" to commit to one person right now. Date multiple people. Yes, it's okay. You just got out of a committed relationship. If you jump into another relationship, you may end up with the same type of partner you just broke up with.

2. Set Your Boundaries.

I learned to do this over time. In fact, I am still learning how to do this properly. I realized once I started getting back out to date, I needed to do it my way. For example, I am not a bar-type girl. I tried to be the fun girl who spent time going to bars and yelling over other people to talk, but that's not me. When I came home, I would be exhausted and disappointed. I went outside of my boundaries because friends thought I would have fun. I didn't. I would rather be at a dinner talking to one person then screaming over ten to be heard. Set your boundaries. If you know something is not for you, don't do it. Don't let yourself be led around because you feel other people know what is better for you. This is your time. Take it to decide how you want your life to look and who you want in it.

3. Jump Online.

Online dating can be a full-time job if you are doing it right; if you are recently divorced and you want to get back out and date or at least meet some good people, though, it can be a great way to connect. Recently, I met a woman who told me that she has at least three new guy friends she met online over the years, so it can work, even if every date is not your soul mate.

The New Single's Cyber Dating Rules

Let's look at some of the things to keep in mind if you are planning to go online for the first time after your divorce. Find someone at your office, or a friend who has done it before, to tell you what she learned from trial and error and a few of the online dating sites she recommends. After you build your profile, here are a few tips to keep in mind while you are learning how to navigate the world of cyber dating.

Make sure you are aware of some of the basic rules of online dating. I once talked to a woman who was seeking dating advice. She told me that she had been divorced for about a year and she was "all good" with it. The only problem was she wanted to meet someone because her girls were going off to college and her husband was marrying the woman he had cheated with. Needless to say, she was dating fast and furious and not doing anything but bringing on what was going to be more hurt down the line. Nevertheless, we sat down to talk about why all the men she was meeting never called for a second date, or called at the last minute, or asked to jump in bed within the first thirty minutes of getting to know her.

I asked her to open up her online account for me and talk me through some of the men she was meeting online. First, she was on a paid site, which I always recommend because there is a minor investment in it (even if it is only a small amount of money) to be able to meet people. Then, we started going through the men and her texts and e-mails between her and the guys. One after another—dirty talk, meet up the night of, drinks only, all conversations that had nothing to do with anything longer term than a few simple strokes of the keyboard.

I was shocked, not by the sexting or messaging or the behavior. I was shocked by the fact she was actually perplexed that a man who was asking her for a hookup in the afternoon was not calling her for a date the next weekend. She seriously believed (and she was fifty-one so there were no excuses) that she was "dating" in order to attract someone long term.

Ladies, I will address and readdress this over and over again. If you want a man past that moment, DO NOT jump into bed with him. If you do, plan on saying goodbye and meaning it. On either side, if it doesn't take effort, it is sending them the message that "it ain't worth it." With that said—and I will say it again—it's essential for you to know what you are dealing with out there. If it is your first time back out in the dating world, I also have some advice for you.

1. Avoid the time suckers at all cost. You can go back and forth talking to someone for days or weeks. Don't bother. Get offline and in person as quickly as possible.

Spend a little time online getting to know the person, but not weeks. This is not to say you need to run out and meet the person that night, but make sure it's no more than seven days before you meet in person. Otherwise, all you have is a pen pal, not a date.

2. No "night of" meetings. This should go without saying, but sometimes people can be anxious. You should not go out and meet someone the first night. Often people are online to hook up. If you are there for a relationship or to meet a person for a date, do not go out and meet someone the night you start communicating. It is not only a bit dangerous; it's simply not smart.

A woman I have known for some time came to me all excited about the fact she was meeting men online. Each week she was showing me pictures of new men she met. She would stay late at work, waiting for them to call or let her know where to meet them. She was hooking up with them after work, during work, and on the weekends simply because she thought that if they showed interest, they were genuinely interested.

I am not a man, but I certainly understand the male mind from working with so many male clients. These men wanted to jump into bed. So, she would go meet them, engage, feel wanted for the moment, and then have to start all over again the next day to feel good about herself. It was becoming a vicious cycle, but one so many successful women believe they can handle. After all, she was running a seventy-five-person department, making close to half a million dollars a year, and raising two girls.

She was convinced she could handle her dating life like she handled her employees. The problem was, she couldn't. No one can. In time, we talked it out. It turns out that her husband left her for a younger woman and she felt old and unattractive and the attention made her feel pretty if just for that small amount of time. It took a lot of phone calls and late-night girl therapy sessions for her to finally stop meeting men for one-night stands. Figure out what *you* need from online dating and don't be the answer to someone's need for cheap thrills.

3. Don't be afraid to insist on a photo with a date on it. This is not to be shallow. The last thing you need to do is plan for a date and then find out the person sent you a picture from ten years ago. *This happens all the time.* Assume everyone you meet is lying about their age and their income—because in all likelihood, they could very well be. Be honest about what you want and, hopefully, you will attract someone doing the same.

4. Speaking of honesty, don't you lie just because everybody else is. It is not attractive to lie, but more important, it's a waste of energy. Changing your age, the city you live in, or your likes and dislikes to attract someone is a waste of everyone's time. Keep it simple. Keep it real. One of the women I spoke with told me her profile said she was forty-five instead of fifty-three because she didn't want an "old man" and didn't want to feel like a "cougar." So, she lied on her profile. She lied on her first dates. In time, she realized she felt awful. After dating this way with no success for about six months, she came clean about her age. She is offline now, because she met someone a few years older who loves the fact that she is not young and that she is a real woman who is not embarrassed about who she is.

5. Do your homework. It is okay to make sure things add up. There are so many stories of people who use the keyboard to make themselves something they are not. If you have the time, check them out on social media. Ask for their place of employment, do some research. You are allowed to do that and more important, you should.

6. Move on if you must. If there is no chemistry, move on. Don't try to spare his feelings by prolonging something that you know is not going to work. Be honest and upfront about it. Everyone will be grateful in the end.

7. Give fellow daters a chance. If you liked the person the first time, but didn't fall in love, schedule a second date to see if something has changed. People can be nervous on the first outing; if you think he has potential, give him a second round.

8. Drop "disappointment" from your vocabulary. Dating online is a numbers game in some ways. Don't be discouraged if you go on ten coffee dates and only like one person. Plan it that way. Meet as many people as you can and see what happens. But, try not to give up and feel down about it. You are out there. It is a huge step back into the world postbreakup.

NINE THINGS YOU SHOULD NEVER LIE ABOUT

I know it's tempting. I know that it's not always easy to come clean upfront when you are trying to make an amazing first impression, but there are simply some critical things you cannot lie about. For the self-help critics, I am sure the next thought is: so you are saying you can lie about some things? No. No. No. But if you have any intention of fibbing, hiding, or disclosing at a later date—avoid the below.

1. Age

It's too difficult to keep track. And eventually the truth comes out.

2. Your job

Not your dream job. Not the one you just applied for. The one that is currently sending you a paycheck.

3. Your true relationship status

Divorce means papers are signed. It doesn't mean we are living together but have been talking about separating.

4. Pets

He could have allergies.

5. Height

Unless you plan on dating him via the Internet forever, don't bother to lie about this one, especially if you prefer heels to flats.

6. Interests

Please don't pretend you are okay camping when in reality your idea of roughing it is the Ritz-Carlton.

7. Whether or not you smoke

Unless you have been wearing the patch for two years, please don't pretend you don't smoke. Lying about it is more of a turnoff for nonsmokers than doing it.

8. Whether you have roommates

I know things can be tough financially, but you need to 'fess up to this one. He will know in time if it's a one-way street to his house only.

9. What you are looking for

If you are looking to date, don't tell him you would be fine with a casual fling. It's not him who will suffer in this; *it's you*. Focus on what you want—don't conform constantly in order to try and get it.

A-TEAM FEATURE

The Truth About Online Dating

Julie Spira is one of America's top online dating experts and digital matchmakers. She's also the founder of CyberDatingExpert .com and shares some important wisdom about digital dating here. Over forty million singles have used online dating sites. With that said, I decided to add a few cyber dating rules to this chapter. I think it's essential for you to know what you are dealing with out there.

WHAT'S THE BEST WAY TO CREATE A PROFILE? FOR A NEWLY DIVORCED WOMAN WHO MAY NOT HAVE DATED IN A LONG TIME, WHAT TIPS DOES SHE NEED TO KNOW WHEN COMPILING A PROFILE?

When you're first getting divorced, you might feel insecure about putting yourself out there. Know that you're not alone and that many others who have been in long-term relationships and marriages are finding themselves in the same boat. There's no better way to get back into the dating scene after your friends stop fixing you up than by joining an online dating site.

The best advice I have is to be confident, genuine, and authentic. So many women feel insecure that they won't fit into a search by the type of man they'd like to meet and they fall into the trap of knocking five years off their age and ten pounds off their weight. While most men are used to this trick, I urge you to be honest about your age and post recent photos. It's too easy to verify this information on other social networks, so starting off your new life and relationship on an honest note is the best path for success in a new relationship. Please remember that your shelf life doesn't have an expiration date. I have worked with couples who have found love and marriage online in their seventies and couldn't be happier.

Since it's time for a new chapter, take the time to update your wardrobe and pick out a great first-date dress for your profile photo. It should be a dress with color, and one that makes you feel the sexiest, without revealing too much. Change up your hairstyle and get ready for a large bouquet of wonderful men that will be happy to be in your company. See below for more on your profile photo.

Don't focus on the fact that you've just gotten divorced. You can list it as your status in your profile and your potential date will know. You're not alone in this arena. To attract a great guy you need to have a positive attitude and leave the baggage at home. Everyone deserves a second or third chance at love and this is the easiest way to get back into the dating game.

WHERE DO YOU START WITH ALL THE NEW APPS?

With all of the new mobile dating apps, singles are now swiping right to give a digital "thumbs up" and swiping left to take a pass on potential dates in a split second. Sure, it seems superficial just to look at a photo and make a decision about someone's character and compatibility, but is it right?

We're living in an instant gratification world with online dating and it's so simple to find a date twenty-four hours a day, but I caution singles on filling up their date card too fast. Take the time to get to know someone through several e-mail exchanges and phone calls before you put a date on the calendar to make the most of your time.

I also suggest that singles who're really looking for a meaningful relationship take the time to utilize all of the features of many of these mobile apps and dating sites, including reading profiles thoroughly, "liking" their photos, seeing who has viewed you, finding out which friends you have in common on Facebook, and also noticing what shared interests you have before taking a pass just based on a photo.

Most of the online dating sites have a mobile-only app, which makes the user experience more enjoyable and more instant. No longer will you need to go home to your desktop computer to create a profile or respond to that cute guy that you have a digital crush on. Many of these mobile apps allow you to sign up through

Facebook and use your Facebook photos in your profile, so it's simpler than ever to connect your social networks and your dating profiles.

For those concerned about mobile dating and texting being solely for those who want to hook up, make sure that your profile is very specific about your relationship goals. After a divorce, some want to date as many people as possible to get back in the game, where others are truly looking for a serious and monogamous relationship. I encourage singles to be honest about their goals to attract a like-minded person. Never be afraid of scaring someone away by saying you're looking for a serious relationship. You really are looking to find that one in forty million.

How do you decide what service to use if you're new to online dating?

There are thousands of online dating sites to pick from and the process can be overwhelming. Most singles join more than one site, typically two to three, with one being a large site with millions of members, a free site, and a niche site such as one based on religion or dietary habits. If you're just dipping a toe in, I suggest joining one of the larger free dating sites such as Plentyof-Fish or OkCupid and a large paid dating site such as eHarmony or Match.com.

What about a photograph? What's the most appealing photo?

Designer Bill Blass had a famous quote, "When in doubt, wear red." I believe this is an absolute must for an online dating profile photo for a few reasons. First, red is the color of love and romance. Second, red is the color of passion. Third, red sends the message to stop and look. If you post a primary photo wearing a little black dress, what would make your photo more unique than every other one? Not much. Researchers from the University of Rochester also found that men will spend more money on a date who is wearing the color red and think that someone wearing red will be more romantic. Need I say more? There's a reason there's magic around "The Lady in Red."

Make sure your primary photo is a headshot and smile into the camera. Let your potential date see your sparkling and inviting eyes. This isn't the time to get artsy. He needs to imagine his life with you and visualize what it might be like holding you in his arms. Also include a full-body shot, because if you do not, men will assume you are a tub of lard.

Avoid group photos, as it can be confusing to a man. He'll wonder which person he will be dating or may think that you're just a party girl. Either way, he's on a dating site to meet one person in a profile, you! Remember to ditch the "selfie" photos. While they're the big trend and fun to take, they really don't show you at your best.

HOW DOES SHE JUDGE THE MEN WHO REACH OUT TO HER?

Know that everyone puts their best digital foot forward when they contact you in an initial e-mail. If the person doesn't have a photo, chances are he isn't serious or want you to see what doesn't he looks like. A man with no photo in his profile is either married or is in a relationship but is looking for a backup plan. Not posting a photo is a big red flag. Look at profiles to see what age range the men you are viewing are seeking. If you're fiftysomething and he's looking for someone twenty-eight to thirty-five, he's not worth pursuing.

See if you think their lifestyle aligns with yours. Not everyone needs to be attached at the hip, but if he's a pure vegan and you love going to steakhouses, it might not work. If he loves camping and hates to travel internationally and your passport is your best friend, you just might not be a match. If he says he's looking for something casual and you know you'd like to have a serious relationship, believe him! Don't try to change him. You can find someone else who is looking for a committed relationship. If he has four dogs and you're allergic to animals, it could be challenging as a couple. Get the point?

WHAT DOES SHE HAVE TO BE CAREFUL ABOUT WHEN ENTERING THE ONLINE WORLD OF DATING?

The goal of online dating is to find someone to meet offline. If someone stalls in making plans to meet with you in a reasonable time, such as within the first few weeks, they might not be available for a relationship, or are juggling too many women. Always avoid talking about your ex-husband on a date. It's so easy to go down that path. If your date says, tell me about your divorce, just change the subject and say, maybe I'll tell you on our tenth date and laugh about it. He'll get the point. Remember that online dating is a numbers game. You need to play to win. As much as women want to be pursued by men and men love the chase, it's best to be proactive as a member of an online dating site.

The reason that online dating fails for many is that they aren't taking a proactive approach to the process. If you just post a few photos, a bio, and who your perfect date should be and wait for someone to find you, your date card won't be filling up fast. Women need to understand that everyone's digital dating patterns vary. Some men will only read e-mails from women and don't use all of the features of the sites. Others only look at photos.

These people may not look to see who has viewed them, hotlisted them, winked, flirted, or liked their photos. Dating is a two-way street. Men are trained to be the pursuers, but when they get frustrated by not receiving responses online from women, they slack off a bit. When women take a passive approach to online dating, it simply just doesn't work. Some women have a hard time finding a date because they post a beautiful profile and sit and wait. Even though finding love is a priority, women need to take matters into their own hands.

Many dating sites have sophisticated algorithms. The only way these algorithms work to help you find a compatible date is to make sure you are an active user of the dating site. Simply put, the more often you log on, the more data the site receives on your likes, dislikes, and communications. Match.com says their users who have met someone sent 30 percent more likes, favorited 26 percent more users, and responded to 3 to 7 percent more messages than users who have not met someone online.

WHERE IS THE BEST PLACE (AND TIME) FOR A FIRST DATE WITH AN ONLINE SUITOR?

Everyone's idea of a perfect first date varies. Some like coffee dates, others can't stand the idea of only meeting for coffee. Others like to meet for drinks and appetizers. If he leaves the restaurant suggestion up to you, remember that men traditionally pay for first dates, so don't select the most expensive restaurant in town to break the bank. He'll think you're high maintenance.

Keep it simple and find a place where you can talk to get to know each other. The goal of a first date is to see if you have enough chemistry or common interests to put a second date on the calendar. I recommend that you suggest a few different ideas. Chances are you won't get to know your date very well if you decide to go to a movie or the theater. There are several free outdoor concerts and art exhibitions that make a first date comfortable and welcoming.

I believe it's always best to schedule a date sooner rather than later. Remember if you're communicating with someone, you're both members of an online dating site and they are also communicating to others. Don't wait around and play hard to get, because the only thing the man will remember is the word "hard" and being with a woman who could be difficult will send your profile to the delete bin fast.

WHAT IF THERE'S NO CHEMISTRY?

More often than not, there isn't the same chemistry offline that you might have shared with your date online. Know that this is common. Instead of frowning through your date, get to know your date. Perhaps he has a friend he can introduce you to. I always believe in casting a wide net, so he might have a good business contact, invite you to a fun party, or become a friend. Let your date know that you enjoyed the conversation, but that you don't think you have enough in common for a romantic relationship. Offer to introduce him to a friend of yours if you know of someone. He'll appreciate your honesty instead of telling him to call you, when you don't really mean it.

WHAT IF THERE IS CHEMISTRY?

Having that chemistry is oh so exciting. However, before you start projecting to the future and thinking he will become your boyfriend or husband, take a deep breath and take the time to get to know him. Chances are he'll be imagining you without your clothes on anyway, because men are visual. A man will wait until you are ready to become intimate, so don't think you have to jump into bed sooner than you want to in order to maintain or deepen your relationship. The fun part about getting to know someone is the courtship stage. Enjoy this time and just date until you decide whether you want to date exclusively or not.

Make sure at the end of the date to let your date know that you had a great time and look forward to seeing him again. This way, he will know for sure that he won't be rejected when he calls or texts. When he does send a text to say he had a great time, don't play hard to get. Send a fun flirty text back to him to keep the communication going. It's digital foreplay at its best.

Online—in Trouble

I was talking to a woman I met recently at a networking evening in New York City. We were talking about this book and, as it often does, the conversation brought about a feeling of comfort to be able to talk openly about divorce, dating, and daring to be happily single. She told me she dedicated herself to being a mom when she and her husband ended their fifteen-year marriage.

At the time her son was ten years old. Once he turned sixteen she decided to start dating. She went online with an amazing profile, written from the heart. As a writer, she was experienced at expressing her feelings. As a new dater, not so experienced at vetting people looking, or in her case allegedly looking, for love. Her story is not an unusual one, but it is a poignant one. After several unfulfilling dates, lots of fun ones, and one longer-than-usual relationship round, she found a person she believed was the real deal.

Handsome.

Four dogs (yes four).

Widowed.

Sensitive.

Smart.

Attentive.

Prince Charming.

Two months and way too many e-mails later she was no longer corresponding with the man on the other end of the dating profile, she was now corresponding with the FBI. Prince Charming turned out to be trying to charm her out of her money. A scam artist who had every bit of information he needed from a vulnerable online match looking for love. Embarrassed, she told me that she was so lonely, she couldn't stand it and would believe anything.

"Facebook Official"

Facebook Official is basically the stage of a relationship that exists somewhere between coupling and engagement. Like digital

PDA. Like wearing your high school boyfriend's letterman jacket or his class ring. Like checking yes/no on a note passed across homeroom. In other words, becoming Facebook Official is a new step in the relationship hierarchy. Unlike past generations in which the loud and proud announcement of a commitment didn't come until the wedding invitations were mailed out, being FBO is the new milestone.

But the thing is this: updating your social network relationship status makes the highs and lows of your love life a matter of public record, at least as far as everyone you know online is concerned. You're a celebrity in your own circle. That's a good thing and a bad thing. First, the good: not long ago, a Facebook research scientist was snooping through your personal life. And he found that a couple who has been FBO for at least three months is likely to go the distance. Well, maybe not the whole distance, but at least four years and maybe longer.

But we're not here because we're all in blissful, Facebook Official relationships. So, let's get real. When you change your relationship status from "in a relationship" or "married" to "single," a LOT of things do and don't happen. First, Facebook will blast it out on all of your friends' news feeds. Hooray. It's like having your own personal "Page Six" delivered right to the iPhones of everyone you even sort of know. Second, and inevitably, you'll have a big percentage of people comment on the change in your status. Or, they'll want to know what happened. To which you think: "As if it's any of their business! FBO?" And third, your real-life friends and coworkers who monitor the news feed non-stop will bombard you with questions right to your face. "Are you okay?" or "Do you need to talk?" Everyone you know knows about your breakup.

You know what doesn't happen, though? Your ex doesn't

automatically disappear into cyberspace. He's still there. Which leads me to another pop-cultural term that you may have heard. Heard? Who am I kidding? I mean, another pop-cultural activity in which we've all partaken: "Facebook stalking."

The thing about social media is that it gives you a direct pipeline into just about everything your ex is doing on any given day. It's like driving by his house to see if he's home. Maybe Facebook stalking saves you that little bit of gas money, but it's actually really emotionally unhealthy. You get trapped in the past.

A recent study by social psychologists at Brunel University found that staying Facebook friends with your ex can really delay the healing process. And it will totally stress you out by leading you on a roller coaster of emotions. Researchers and common sense say you'll get your feelings hurt, you'll get mad, you'll get lonely, and you might start to miss the physical aspects of the relationship (even if it wasn't as good as you remember—and it probably wasn't).

Un-friending won't cut it, either. You've probably got mutual friends. And any time he comments on one of their posts, or posts on one of their timelines, you'll see it. Especially if you're trying to Facebook stalk him. And, of course, there are ghosts of the past still living on your page. Shared photos, posts, and check-ins. So, what to do?

The healthiest move is to take a break from social media. Stay off of Facebook for a while. Uninstall the app from your phone. Or, dare I say it? Click "deactivate." Desperate times call for desperate measures. Leave the cyber world for a while. Deactivate your page. Don't worry; it won't go away forever. Because Facebook is like the Hotel California; "You can check out any time you like, but you can never leave." You can reactivate your page once you're in a better place and a better emotional state.

And speaking of desperate measures, you could also go for the kill, without the violence. A lot of people take breaks from Facebook after ending a relationship, only to eventually come back to find traces and faces of the past there waiting for them. So, there's an app for that. Apps like KillSwitch can delete the Facebook history of your ex from your timeline. They'll remove all pictures, references, and wall posts that you're in with your ex.

Warning Signs. Pay Attention to the Pink Flags

We will call him Dan, just so that all innocent parties are protected, or in this case, not so innocent. Dan owned a bicycle and some clothes when I met him, He was thirty-six and "between jobs." He was living on a friend's couch while he figured out his next steps in life. I ignored all that. Furthermore, he had been married before and admitted he had cheated. Again, I ignored the red flags. He was also a big spender—of funds he did not have. My funds, as it turned out. Red flag number three.

But, he was fun. He loved to jump without nets. He was charming. He was fearless. And, he was everything the person before him was not—so I jumped without nets myself—only to later realize that I had ignored every warning sign out there. I turned the red flags a pretty shade of pink—because I didn't want to see what was in front of me. I wanted to paint the picture my way. I can't count the number of women who do this. It's not because we are all so Pollyanna, but I do believe women for the most part want to believe they can either fix the problems or at least remedy the situation and make it all better. The problem is, we only make it worse by not being honest with ourselves, with what we are looking for and with what will make us happy. Learn from my mistake. Here is what I did when I changed the Red Flags (reality) to Pink Flags (fairy tale).

RED FLAG:

Dan owned a bicycle and some clothes when I met him. Nothing else.

PINK FLAG:

He just went through a divorce. It is not his fault. He gave his ex-wife everything—except the clothes on his back.

RED FLAG:

He was thirty-six years old. He was between jobs.

PINK FLAG:

He said his investor bailed on him. It's not his fault, things happen. He is ambitious. He will come out better for it.

RED FLAG

He was living on someone's couch and he was trying to figure out his next steps in life. Furthermore, he has been married before and admitted he had cheated.

PINK FLAG:

What a nice guy. He gave everything to his ex-wife because he felt so guilty.

This is the kind of man I want—he can admit when he's wrong.

(Yes, I said that.)

RED FLAG:

He was also a spender. A big spender; problem was his funds did not meet the fun that he wanted to have.

PINK FLAG:

We only live once. Anyway, he can make more money and he always has an amazing time. So, why should I always be such a killjoy?

Sounds silly—doesn't it? How many times have you done the exact same thing: looked at a situation and painted a beautiful picture when you really knew the truth. The last thing you want as you get back on the dating scene is to ignore red flags or turn them a pretty shade of pink. Be honest with yourself. Are you kidding yourself about the new person in front of you, just so you have a person? Are you ignoring deal breakers so that you don't feel broken? Are you making Mr. Right Now into Mr. Right just to have a Mr. in your life?

If you can truthfully answer those questions and have answered yes to any of them, you need to think long and hard about what you are doing. The numbers speak for themselves with so many second marriages ending in divorce. Moving on does not mean simply getting over your ex, it means getting to a new phase of your life and the decisions you are about to make for your future.

Here are a few more of the red flags that women turn into pink flags to avoid the truth about a man they want to be with.

RED FLAG:
   The Wandering Eye
PINK FLAG:
   He just likes to flirt. It doesn't mean anything.

Men will be men. Most men notice other women and appreciate a beautiful face or body. But if the man you are on a date with or currently dating goes out of his way to notice a woman, it is a sign of total disrespect. When you are in his presence, you are his present. If he makes you feel insecure or not good enough around him, no matter how wonderful he is, it is a deal breaker.

I have a cousin who is twenty years older than I. We became close after my marriage ended. She is treated like a queen by the men who take her out. They worship her. She is given gifts, taken on trips by men hopelessly devoted to her. She has one belief, "I am the prize." She is from Texas, so she says it with that sweet Texan drawl, but the words are really the sweet part: YOU ARE THE PRIZE. Don't forget that. If you have a man with a wandering eye, you need to wander off as quickly as possible.

RED FLAG:

He works too hard to be Mr. Perfect.

PINK FLAG:

I am the first to believe that chemistry is not just a part of finding the right relationship, it is everything. I love to draw from stories of women who share their dating experiences with me. In this case we will call her Diane. Diane told me she recently went on a date with a guy from Match.com. He was tall, he was in pretty good shape, and he was making good money. Compared to the men she had been out with over the past few months, it was shaping up to be a good night. When he picked her up, he opened the door and was a perfect gentleman. But he was too perfect. In the end it turned out that he was still married and was "dating" because he thought that he was in an open relationship. Only problem was, his wife didn't know.

RED FLAG:

A leopard can change his spots, but not for long.

PINK FLAG:

I truly believe that people can change. In fact, I lived by this motto for many years. The problem is that even if people change, more often than not, they don't change for long—especially when it comes to being unfaithful. I recently had a tough conversation with a friend of mine about cheating. She has been in a relationship with the same man for about six years. She wants to get married. He doesn't. She has accepted that and is happy with the commitment they have. Except now she is not so sure he is keeping his end of the commitment.

We started talking about the signs of cheating. Which, of course, is itself never a good sign. But it got me thinking about whether there are unmistakable signs of infidelity. While no person or relationship is the same, it turns out that there are a few signs that are hard to overlook. I pass them along for your consideration.

HOW TO SPOT A CHEATER

When you start dating someone and something just doesn't feel right, you shouldn't just brush it off. Sometimes you just know. You feel it in your gut. Call it intuition or perhaps it is just something you sense and don't want to admit.

While I hope that you don't ever see any of these signs in a new relationship, these are just a few to help you in case you are having some doubts. Don't take them as law, but do take them seriously because you deserve someone as committed to you as you are to them.

1. He Treats You Differently

Is he suddenly overly attentive? Is this behavior out of character? If you're suddenly receiving gifts from him that you've never gotten before, or he's calling you at unusual times (early in the morning, during work, for example), it may be a pink flag of WHAT? It is great to have all those things if he has always behaved that way. If he hasn't, then you may want to give things a second look.

2. He Treats Himself Differently

If your man is suddenly rocking out to music you have never heard of, wearing a new scent, and is all of a sudden the life of the party it could be a sign there is something else going on in his life. Midlife crisis is always an option, but if that is not the case, he could be straying. Oftentimes, men take on new behavior or the likes of the person they are trying to impress and striving to be with.

3. Accusing You of Things He's Doing

If a person is suddenly accusing you of cheating, this is one of those classic signs of cheating. This can happen because he is overridden with guilt and is projecting his feelings onto you.

4. You Can't Get in Touch With Him

If you do not have access to your partner's phone or he turns it off or is very private and jumpy when it rings, he most likely has something to hide. A man with nothing to hide is not worried about who's calling or worried about turning his phone over so you can't see who is ringing his line.

5. He's Testy and Likes to Argue

It's a strange sign, but it is a sign of cheating. Like the gift giving, this can be due to a high level of guilt and the fact he is trying to excuse himself for his behavior.

He is fighting with you so he can justify the fact he is seeing someone else, because he is not happy in the relationship.

6. Intimacy? What Intimacy?

Your bedroom time together comes to a screeching halt. If you can't remember the last time you were intimate, it could indicate a bigger problem. Don't ignore this sign; it's one of the biggest red flags.

7. The Third Wheel (or something like that)
There is suddenly a new person he is talking about all the time. She just comes up in conversation for no reason at all or as part of a story. We are not talking about once or twice but all the time, even when a story does not need the addition of her name.

The Most Important Rule: Keep Your Bed Empty for 180 Days

No men in your bed for six months. Hate me yet? Please don't. I promise it's not eternity, though I must admit it can feel like it. Six months. One hundred eighty days. Four thousand three hundred twenty hours. Break it down however you like, just don't do it. About a year after I came up with this rule, I appeared on *The Talk* on CBS with Sharon Osborne and the ladies.

The women of *The Talk* were a bit shocked at my rule. I actually jumped out of my seat because Sharon screamed, "One hundred eighty days!!!" When I explained the "why" behind my rule, I think they softened a bit. You need time to know yourself again before you share the new you with another person.

I am not a prude. I get it, you are just out of a relationship and you want to feel attractive again. You want to feel like someone wants you again. But jumping into bed with the first person that shows you attention is not going to feel good in the morning. If you jump into bed with someone on the first date, and then there is no second date, you might just feel like you're reliving that bad breakup all over again!

True story. For months I sat at home on Saturday nights, I ate pizza in my sweats with my Chihuahua on my lap, watching a movie, with no man in sight. I did date, but I kept either my Saturday or Sunday night to myself. The truth is there is something good about being alone. There is nothing worse than being out on a date with someone I don't want to be with and feeling lonely. Think about it. And then order an extra topping on your pizza until you are ready to get back out there.

The New Single in a New Relationship

The first date was great.

So was the second one.

Then you meet some of his friends.

Now you are up to twice a week seeing him.

He's younger than your ex.

Or perhaps, he's a little older.

Could even be shorter than you want.

Maybe no more abs of steel like your former flame (believe me, I've dated the ones who have looked at their own bodies more than they looked at mine).

Regardless of whom you are seeing, you are moving toward a new relationship. And maybe that old status: couple.

So what now? No matter what it looks like in your head or sounds like coming out of your mouth, you must learn that being the New Single is perfect, if not perfectly acceptable. In fact, it may be just what is needed before you can be part of a couple again or perhaps it is what you want for the long term. Either way, listening to those around you and their thoughts about having someone or having a better half is not what you should be concentrating on right now.

Once you appreciate the benefits of being on your own, you

are ready to decide in a healthy way if you want to be part of a couple once again. Each of us has our own lessons from past loves, lovers, or partners. Sometimes we learn more than one. Sometimes we learn that we needed that relationship to move us to our next place in life. And sometimes, we learn boundaries.

A relationship that has ended often helps set up future relationship boundaries. This is a time to be honest about your needs and stick to them. First, you have to stop listening to the naysayers. I have often found that people want you to be like them. They assume that what makes them happy will make you happy. Learn to set boundaries as to what you listen to. Make sure you are not conforming your belief system to match theirs and not listening to what people say about getting back out there. You are going to do that when you are ready and not before that.

If you look at a breakdown of the numbers you will find that two-thirds of second marriages end in divorce and third marriages end 73 percent of the time.

The goal is not to find another person to marry or even to find the perfect partner. The goal is to become comfortable with the person you are now. Then, and only then, can you truly find someone with whom to be happy. As you start dating again and start moving into a new relationship, there are some things to keep in mind. I truly believe that the only goal and end game to moving forward is to be happy and proud to be The New Single.

I (Tamsen) Am Not Your Mom, Sister or Best Friend

Yes, I know you know. I know you are probably wondering why I wrote that. You are about to find out. If you want someone to be real with you—keep reading. I haven't minced any words yet, so

I am not about to start now. In the first few chapters I was clear this book is about rebooting yourself and starting over again to move forward with the life you should be leading now. But, the following love lessons for your next relationship could cause you to roll your eyes or say that I am being old-fashioned or silly. But pay close attention; if you take one piece of the advice or all of it, I think you will be better for it as you enter the next potential relationship. We will call these "Love Lessons."

Love Lessons
Don't Look for the Endgame

I know you are excited about the idea of someone amazing with whom to spend the next Saturday night. Or, you have a wedding to attend and you desperately want to reply "will attend with guest." Or, you are dying to go out to eat at your favorite old restaurant but are intimidated when the hostess makes the truthful observation, "just one tonight"? As tempting as it sounds, it's so important to enjoy NOW. Do not fast-forward to the endgame.

Stay in Your Lane

When we meet someone new, oftentimes we tend to bond by coming together in certain areas and making his problems ours and vice versa. In my case, my former husband was not thrilled about what he was doing at the time we met, so I set out to create a new business for him. In the end, I created the business. I thought it was best for him and for us. In hindsight, however, I am not sure if it *was* best for him at the time. It created a lot of pressure on him and put him in the place that *I* thought was best for him. If you really care about someone, or think you are going to, stay in your lane. Enjoy each other, but don't try to get involved with his whole world too soon and lose yourself in it. Men are not looking for a mommy. Most men, the ones that you should be looking for, want a partner, a girlfriend or a wife. When you find yourself "doing" for him as a mother would do for a child— stop it immediately. It's not only taking away from you, it's turning him away from you as well.

Don't Try to Change a Man

I met one of my former boyfriends through a mutual friend. He was fun. He was older. He was easy to talk to.

He was a confirmed bachelor.

My friend cautioned me to make sure I was really okay with that, because, she said, he was not going to change. He was not looking for love. Period. Stubborn and always convinced I understood the art of persuasion if it needed to be used, I went full steam ahead. At the time, I thought he was just what I needed. I was starting a new job. I just wanted to have fun. I was not looking for anything serious.

One year later, I realized I liked him. A lot. So, I set out to change him. At first in subtle ways, then more deliberate.

Unbeknownst to me, I was not the first woman who set out to do this. It soon became very clear to me that he was the pro at this and I was simply a student of love. It was one of the biggest lessons I learned about men and, truthfully, about people in general. *Do not* try to change people. In the end, they will go back to who they were if they try to change. If they don't, you will end up losing them because they end up losing interest. Think about it. How many people have tried to change you? Have given you advice that you knew would never work for you? Or, have told you when you were going about things wrong? It doesn't work, does it? Well, then do unto others—or rather don't.

Don't Share All of Yourself Too Soon

I know. We don't like to play games. We like to be upfront and tell all. Well, now is not the time to do that. In fact, for a long time, it will not be the time to do that. I am not saying this for the good of the potential relationship—rather I am saying it for the good of you—the New Single. You are a brand-new version of yourself. You have just rebooted your life. You do not need to find the first person out there and then dump all of your baggage, concerns, fears, past problems, or future fiascos on this person the moment you meet them. Be light. Live in the now. Do not keep revisiting the past or trying to predict the future. This is where yoga came in for me. Learning the power of time and the power of now has been an essential part of my healing and my growth. Let it be for you as well.

WHAT TO EX-PECT FROM HIS EX

Here are Florida Supreme Court–certified family law mediator and divorce coach, Diane L. Danois, J.D.'s pointers on your new man's ex. Remember, knowledge is power!

- Expect the ex to immensely dislike you, regardless of the reason or timing of the divorce.

- Expect the ex to take advantage of your good nature, and expect no reciprocity.

- Expect that there will be moments of civility among you, your partner, and the ex, and moments when you can see why they're no longer together.

- Expect that the ex will be in your life for as long as you are in the children's lives. Love it or hate it, your relationship with the ex will likely extend well beyond the child support years.

Do Not Get Physical Too Soon

I dedicated several other areas of the book to this one, but it bears repeating. If you get physical too soon, just plan on him being Mr. Right Now, not Mr. Right. No man wants it all as soon as he thinks he wants it. Keep the 180-day rule in the back of your head. There is a reason it's there. There have been countless studies and facts and figures about how women get attached to a man they are physical with. But, you don't need a study or a cuddle hormone or a scientist to tell you if you move too fast for you it's not going to work. Period.

Go Slowly

Keep the phone calls short. Don't go from zero to sixty in terms of how often you see him. Don't think that everything is urgent. You are newly single. You are not going to get this time back. Usually in a relationship, the beginning is the most exciting. So, try to keep that as long as possible. There is nothing worse than jumping into a new relationship only to find once you are there, you are now trying to figure out a way to get out of it. This is the time to get to know the other person. Imagine it's like a hot bath.

Ease into it. Test it out with your big toe first and then your an-kle, go up to your knees, and then eventually climb all the way in. Picture how relaxing that bath is once you are there. That is exactly how the right relationship should be. Easy to be in. Re-laxing. Enjoyable. Not painful so you want to jump out of it as quickly as you got into it.

Be on Your Time Schedule—Not on the Other Person's

I was sitting down with a friend who was telling me about her new relationship. She had been happily dating a guy who seemed supercool. Fun. Easygoing. Always up for something new. They both had a lot of common interests and their chemistry was in-credible. Problem was, he was five years out of a divorce. She was one year out. He was ready to move in together. She was still trying to remember to say her maiden name again instead of her married one. While we were talking, she mentioned her new boy-friend was talking about the future. A lot.

She rarely said anything about it, because she wasn't ready to. I noticed as our conversation went on, she was trying to con-vince herself that she was further along in the relationship than she really was. You have to be on your own time schedule. You cannot let someone else's love dictate yours. Only you know when you are ready to move to the next step. If you do it too soon, you will both lose. Be prepared to be honest. Perhaps even hurt his feelings initially. But don't lead someone on for fear of losing him or being honest with him. In order to blossom in a relationship, first you have to grow on your own.

Be Okay If It Doesn't Work Out

I hope more than anything in the world the new relationship you are about to embark on is going to work. In fact, I have all the faith in the world that you have set your boundaries, fallen back in love with yourself, and made sure you are ready to be out there again. But, if by chance this coupledom doesn't work out, it is okay. In fact, it is better than okay. Every new person you date or have several dates with will not be the one. It is statistically impossible. It is universally improbable. Enjoy the time. Live in the moment. But be okay if it doesn't work out and you are posting your profile back on Match.com, because it's simply O-K.

Stop Comparing This to Your Old Relationship

It's not easy. In fact, no matter how much time goes by, it is nearly impossible. But if you have any interest at all in moving to the next place in your life, you have to stop comparing the new person to the old person. It seems obvious. We all know it's a bad idea and will never end well. Women are the culprits of this one more than men are. In fact, it seems as if we are almost looking for approval from our new guy to be over our old one. So, we tell stories (good or bad), make comparisons, and ultimately offend the very person we are trying to be with. Bottom line: leave this conversation to have with your mom, sister, or best friend. Just don't have the conversation with him.

Move On If It's Not Working

Time and time again in interviewing people for this book and talking with groups of women about starting over, I have found that many refused to admit when it was not working. Whether it was foolish pride, fear of the unknown, or hope that it was "just a stage," they stayed in the relationship well past the expiration date, and in doing so, lost themselves along the way. If you are in a relationship or a dating scenario that is not working, don't worry about what other people will think or how difficult it is going to be to get out of it—just get out. Moving on is the kindest thing you can do for someone rather than stay somewhere that you don't want to be. False pride has no place in a relationship. Leave it at the door so that you can decide where you want to be.

Where Do I Go to Meet People?

The New Single life means it's time to knock some more of the old clichés out of your mind. Which means changing your thought process on where to meet a man. Men are everywhere. It's not hard to meet a man. Jerry Seinfeld used to joke: "Wherever women are, we have a man on the situation right now." In the same joke, he says men get frustrated when they see women reading articles or books (like this one) on how to meet men because men really are everywhere. The problem, of course, is how do you find, pick, and snag a good one? Where do you go?

The old dating books and just about every sitcom on television tell us that the supermarket is a prime spot to meet a mate. But think about how you dress to get the groceries. Yoga pants and a concert T-shirt from 1997. We're turning into sloppier shoppers. And men are just as bad. When is the last time you actually saw a well-dressed man thumping melons at D'Agostino's? If it was any time in the past five years, then he was the exception. (Note: if you are convinced this is the best option, don't go when it's busy. As counterproductive as that sounds, men HATE busy supermarkets.)

Do you have a Kindle? Or did you order this book online? Exactly. That's why you're not nearly as likely to find your own true love at the bookstore anymore, either.

And forget the club scene; save that for Iggy Azalea.

So, where to go? Here are FIVE actual places to go to meet quality people.

1. Your Favorite Museum. Mine is the MoMA. Why is this good? Because he's at a museum! And if he's there (and he's single), it means one of two things. He's cultured, or at least trying to be. And it's a safe bet that he's also literate. Or, the other scenario is that he's there to meet you. And even if he's not into German Expressionism, he's smart enough to know to go to a museum to meet a cultured woman. In any case, he's probably not dragging his knuckles.

2. The Apple Store. It's the new bookstore. And with more than 250 Apple stores in the US, it's becoming the perfect environment for meeting a potential new Mr. Perfect. If you want a techy guy, you can take a workshop in how to use your new Mac or iPad. A musician? A GarageBand workshop. Or an amateur filmmaker? Take the quick iMovie workshop.

3. The Dog Park. I know, I know; it's so *Sex and the City*. But there's a lot of truth in fiction. Your four-legged family member can also be your matchmaker. You can do this organically by taking your little monkey to the park. Or there are social meet-up and dating sites for pet owners. In New York City, it's Leashes and Lovers. Your city might just have a similar option.

One more note about this. My dog is a little monster, which I adore. But he's not the most dog-park-social creature. So, also try a pet obedience class.

4. Your Favorite Restaurant. I love Bar Pitti. It's a restaurant in the West Village that has outdoor seating in the summer and it always makes me happy to go there. The food is great. The people are fun. And, it's wonderful for people watching. I am comfortable and not self-conscious about sitting down for a meal by myself. Therefore, I can easily meet people because it is not a forced situation. Try picking your head up from your phone or computer and look around at your favorite restaurant. You might find a nice selection not on the menu.

5. The Gossip Mill. Sounds strange? Don't worry, it's a not-so-odd bar where people stand around and talk about each other. And, I'm not talking about your office. This is about TELLING people you are single. Everyone, in fact. Gossip about it. Let them gossip about it. Tell them to tell a friend. And then use that gossip for your better good. Allow people to make introductions. It only has to be for coffee or for a quick drink. Meet people. Stay friends or go for a second date or trash their number if it's that bad of a date. But make sure your name is out there.

Before You Say "I Do" Again

I said it at the beginning and I will say it again. I love love. I hope for you that if you want to say the words "I do," again you will do just that. I love to see couples walking down the streets like no one else is there. Or people being okay just talking and not having to work on their phones or Tweet just to get through a meal together. But if there is anything that I want to impress upon you—it's time. Before you say "I do" again to someone else, say it a few times to yourself.

I do love myself.

I do know that I am capable of handling anything.

I do know that I am enough.

I do accept I am beautiful.

I do make right choices.

I do trust myself.

I do feel happy when I am alone.

I do know that I am strong.

I do know that I am confident.

I do remain open to love.

We Don't Need a Fairy-Tale Ending to Be Happy

Everything happens for a reason.

I was married in *The New York Times*.

I was divorced in the *New York Post*.

On May 12, 2014, an article came out that I was going to pen a book on my messy divorce. Essentially, it was a brief rehash of the less-than-stellar moments that brought me to this point—and a footnote to the world that I was writing another book. If you've made it this far, you hopefully know that this hasn't been some salacious tell-all. But guess who didn't love to hear that?

My ex-husband.

His new girlfriend.

I spent the better part of that day battling a barrage of angry phone calls and text messages from my ex about the fact he thought I was going to be digging up the past.

But the specific date this happened, May 12, 2014, is important for a reason.

That night, I had to attend a media event for work. It was the grand reopening party for Tavern on the Green. May 12, 2014.

You know how I said I was married in *The New York Times*? Well, in 2007 I was married at Tavern on the Green. The *Times* covered it. Tavern closed in 2008. And after a four-year hiatus, it was back in business nestled right there at the corner of Central Park. And there I was, on opening night, back at the very place I was married, on the very day I was reminded of the life that I'm thankful I no longer have. If I was looking for one more sign that it was time to keep moving forward and stop looking back, the Tavern on the Green sign with the two sheep and the crown was it. Now that's poetic.

If my ex reads this he will discover that I have no interest in ruining his life or anyone else's. In fact, the point has been to illustrate how much better my life has become, and how much better it continues to get. The point is self-empowerment. Accepting your New Single life. Making yourself priority number one for the first time in a long time. Learning to relove yourself before you try and learn to love anyone else. Making peace with the past. And moving forward. Always moving forward. My favorite words of wisdom from my father are: "It's better to be alone than lonely with someone else." They are words that I live by. I hope you will, too.

Appendix A

Q & A: Tamsen Tackles Your Tough Questions

I am into him, and he seems to be into me, so why can't I just shower him with attention?

Three ways to lose a man quickly:

1. Be constantly available.

2. Consult or consider him before every decision.

3. Always talk about the future.

This is so hard for women because we don't want to waste any time with a guy that doesn't have the same future plans as us. We need to know! Trust me. I wasted plenty of time with guys who led me to "believe" they were the one, so I went with it, only to learn the hard way. Plus, why does the guy always determine the time frame? Our wants and needs are also relevant in the relationship. Go as far as you feel comfortable, but don't overdo it too soon. In other words, don't buy him expensive gifts, spend all your precious time with him, or cater to his every whim unless you're getting the same attention in return, or unless you can handle it if it's not reciprocated.

He says he doesn't want children. Could he change his mind?

I don't want to get your hopes up, but some men do change their minds about children when they meet the right woman. So, his no-kids-policy announcement may be his way of telling you that you are not the right one for him. He may not even *realize* what is going on himself—until he meets Miss Right. Then, all of a sudden, children are in the picture. But, if he is certain he doesn't want children and you are sure you do, then getting serious with someone like that is not only not an option, it is simply not smart. Don't go into a relationship starting with a list of ways you are going to need to change someone. It's bad for him and worse for you.

Should I date a married man? He says he and his wife are unhappy and they will eventually divorce.

For a woman like you who is used to being in control of her life, it must be extremely frustrating to wait for this guy to make up his mind and leave his wife. Never forget that the past and present are good indicators of the future. He will continue to enjoy your company until you have the guts to call it quits, at which time he will find another mistress and give her the same story. The number of men who leave the comfort of their wives for "the other woman" is extremely small. Start looking at your personal life as you do your business life. Would you put up with this kind of behavior in a business deal? Most likely, you have never settled professionally, so why settle personally? Get out now and start looking for a man who is not in a relationship so he can have one with you.

My ex is getting married. We were together for eight years and he has only known her for eighteen months. How do you cope with this without losing confidence?

It happens. Quite often, in fact. It doesn't mean that he was not into you. It doesn't mean he didn't love you. In fact, it has nothing to do with you. Sometimes people move from one place into another in their lives and it has to do with timing. Don't run to her Facebook page and try to figure out what she has that you don't. There will be nothing there. Accept the fact that he has moved on and it was his time. Soon it will be yours, too. I recently spoke with two women who told me they had to deal with their exes remarrying. It was painful. In fact, it was nearly impossible for them to look at me when they were talking. It's okay. But, it's not okay if you don't release the past and move forward to create positive change in your life.

Is it okay to ask a man about his past?

It is always okay but not always helpful. What do you need to know? More important, *why* do you need to know it? If he has been married three times, that tells you that he may not be great at relationships or at least not great at picking the right people for him. If he is fifty and has never been married, it tells you he has not met the one and perhaps isn't willing to do that or to settle down. Give it time. Allow it to play out naturally. Of course, don't be silly about it; know who you are going out with, but don't investigate his past to figure out your future.

Are men intimidated by women who make more money than they do?

Some men are, but that is not something you can think about. You have to be yourself. If you are, you will attract a like-minded person and the money you make won't be a contest, rather it will just be a fact. And, if he is the right person with the right intentions, it will not be an issue. Just make sure you are not taking over in the dating stages and making him feel inadequate because you have more money than he does. Allow him to take you to places within his budget and not expect to go to places that will make him feel strained.

Is it okay to date a younger man?

Yes. As long as you are doing it for the right reasons and as long as you have enough in common to keep you both interested. Whether you go up or down in age make sure there are enough things you both share to be able to enjoy one another in all aspects of the relationship, *if* you are looking for one.

My ex and I are still friendly. Can I call him just to talk?

If you share children or have a financial issue to discuss, then e-mail him. If and only if it's a real emergency should you be calling him to talk—especially during the workday. You are not in a relationship with him anymore. He is your *former* boyfriend, husband, or partner.

He calls, but never when he says he's going to. I don't have time to play games. So, should I just decide the time and place for our dates?

I don't care what your shrink, your friends, or your coworkers tell you. It's not about playing games. It's about setting parameters. You start setting them the minute you make eye contact and/or say hello to each other. If you want to forever be the person who decides the time and place, takes charge, and acts like the man, be my guest. But I am here to tell you this guy probably won't be around for long. Most men want to at least believe they are in control, even though I think deep down they know they aren't. Let him make the plans, and if he doesn't then he wasn't really interested in the first place. Let him make the call, and if he doesn't, it's not because he was too busy, it's because you are not and may never be his priority.

I would like to ask a guy out. Is that okay?

At the risk of sounding old-school, I worry that asking a guy out will start a precedent that puts you in the driver's seat. Be open with him and you can hint at spending time together, but asking a man out means that you may be doing everything moving forward and leading the potential relationship. If he wants to ask you out, he will. I have yet to meet a man so shy he cannot ask a woman out if he wants to get to know her better.

Is it okay to date a guy for money?

I find it funny that women ask that question. The ones that ask already know the answer. The ones that don't ask also know the answer, but have made a different decision in their lives. I am happy with what makes you happy, but don't date someone for money hoping that the love will come down the road. I am not saying you have to choose one or the other, but always be honest with yourself about what you are doing.

How do I stop obsessing over a guy that I went out with?

Technology is great when it comes to staying in touch. Technology is not so great when you don't want to. Looking at your phone every thirty seconds, checking your e-mails and hoping for a text message won't make someone come around any faster. If you sent him a text or e-mail and haven't gotten a response, please, please, *please* don't send another to see if he got the first one. Put down your phone, let him respond to you, and don't obsess if and when he sends one back.

Is it wrong to assume that a man will be monogamous after I first start dating him?

Yes. You need to realize that you are "dating." That means until you have spent significant time together or really gotten to know one another, he is most likely playing the field. And you should be, too. Do not assume because you have had four fabulous dates that his profile should come down off of Match.com and he should start thinking about drawer space. Please give yourself the space you need as you embark on this new journey.

Appendix B

The New Single's Workout Log

Exercise	Weight	Reps	Sets
BACK AND BICEPS DAY			
FOR THE BACK			
one-armed rows	10–15 lbs	10–12	3
front lateral pull downs	30–35 lbs	10–12	3
seated rows	40–45 lbs	10–15	3
FOR THE BICEPS			
bicep curls standing (alternate)	8–10 lbs	10 each arm	3
cable curls	10–15 lbs	10–12	3
SHOULDERS, CHEST AND TRICEPS DAY			
FOR THE SHOULDERS			
side lateral dumbbell raise	8 lbs	15–20	3
front dumbbell raise	5 lbs	15–20	3
upright dumbbell raise	10 lbs	15	3

(continued)

Exercise	Weight	Reps	Sets
alternate dumbbell shoulder press	10 lbs	10 each arm	3

FOR THE CHEST

flat dumbbell press	12 lbs	10–15	3
chest flys	8 lbs	10–15	3
inclined dumbbell press	10 lbs	12–15	3

FOR THE TRICEPS

standing tricep push-downs	25 lbs	12–15	
triceps bench dip	body weight	10–12	3
behind-the-neck tricep press	12 lbs	10–12	3

THE LOWER BODY DAY

walking lunges	body weight	10 each leg	3
squats	body weight	15	3
side lateral leg lifts	body weight	15	3
fire hydrants	body weight	10 each leg	3

FOR CARDIO

3–4 × A WEEK

30 minutes on treadmill or elliptical

10 incline / 2 speed

FOR THE ABS - I DO ON ALL DAYS

ab curbs on the ball		25	4

*my favorite

Appendix C

The New Single's Yoga With Mike McArdle

My love of yoga runs deep. I look forward to each and every class and cherish the time that there are no cell phones, computers, or social media sites to post to. I hope that whatever exercise you love to do, you will take the time out of your busy schedule to love yourself as a New Single and remember you can only love someone else once you learn to appreciate YOU.

LOWER BODY:

Chair pose. 30 seconds.
Step back with right leg.
High lunge. Bend leg/ straighten leg—5×.
    After the 5 repetitions, come back to high lunge and hold for 30 seconds; from high lunge, lower back leg to a low lunge. Arms up. Hold right wrist with left hand and side bend to left. 30 seconds.
Roll to the outer edge of left foot, open knee, and with palm
    push the thigh away. 30 seconds.
(This side will take roughly 2½ to 3 minutes.)

REPEAT THE WHOLE SEQUENCE ON THE OTHER SIDE.

UPPER BODY:

Plank pose, floss shoulders. 30 seconds.

Down dog/up dog/chaturanga 5 × 30 to 60 seconds.

Down dog roll to side plank, right side to left side. Repeating for 10x—1 minute.

Donkey kicks (kicking heels to butt with bent knees) 30 reps—1 minute.

Quadruped. Take right arm up, twist right. 30 seconds.

Wrap arm around left waist to bind.

Release arm back up.

Thread arm through across body to left from front chest.

REPEAT THE WHOLE SEQUENCE ON THE LEFT SIDE.

Come back to the belly. Place DT under upper right chest (pectoral).

Turn DT 20 degrees right. Extend right arm overhead, relax arm, tent fingers and engage right arm. Repeat 5×.

Switch to left side and repeat. Total of 2 minutes for this exercise.

CORE WORK:

Lie on back. Bring legs to tabletop. Place hands on midthighs. Isometric resistance: push hands to thighs, thighs to hands.

For more resistance, lift head, shoulders, and shoulder
blades off the floor.
Release feet to floor, press up to bridge to stretch front body.
10 seconds.
Take hands to right knee, extend left leg 30 degrees off floor.
Again, for more resistance lift head, shoulders, and
shoulder blades off the floor.

REPEAT LEFT SIDE

Release feet to floor, press up to bridge to stretch front body.
10 seconds.
Sit up with feet on the floor. Balance on left outer glute, float
feet off floor. Reach arms to the right. Lean back left with
torso.
Lower down as far as possible lengthening body; pull back on
exhale.
Switch sides and repeat 10×.
Cross ankles, fold forward 5 breaths then roll up to sit.

The New Single Experts

A heartfelt thank-you to the New Single Experts who helped fill the pages of this book with so much incredible information and amazing tips. I have learned so much from these special people and I am so proud to be able to share their advice with you. I encourage you to visit their Web sites and follow them on social media. Their daily advice has worked wonders for me and I hope it does the same for you.

Amy Acton, celebrity stylist, www.stylestudio.tv

Toby Amidor, MS, RD, national nutrition expert and author of *The Greek Yogurt Kitchen: More Than 130 Delicious, Healthy Recipes for Every Meal of the Day*, (Grand Central Publishing, 2014)

Diane Danois, attorney and Florida Supreme Court–certified family law mediator, www.dianedanois.com

Keri Gans, MS, RDN, CDN, nutrition consultant, speaker, and author of *The Small Change Diet*, www.kerigansnutrition.com

Judy Goss, founder and CEO of Over 40 Females, www.over40females.com and www.judygoss.com

Jen Groover, serial entrepreneur, author, motivational speaker, and host of PBS's *Empowered*, www.jengroover.com

Cathy Hobbs, interior designer and home staging, www.cathyhobbs.com

Dr. Diana Kirschner, psychologist and author of *Find Your Soulmate Online in 6 Simple Steps, 30 Days to Love, Sealing the Deal: The Love Mentor's Guide to Lasting Love,* and *Love in 90 Days,* founder of www.lovein90days.com

Dr. Shirley Madhere, New York City holistic plastic surgeon and owner of
Jet Set Beauty Rx, www.thenewaesthete.com

Sherri Mathieson, style consultant and author of *Forever Cool* and *Steal
This Style*, www.sherriemathieson.com

Linda Meaney, New York City psychotherapist

Andrew Mellen, organizational expert and author of *Unstuff Your Life!*
www.andrewmellen.com

Mike McArdle, New York City yoga instructor, www.michaelmcardleyoga
.com

Melanie Notkin, founder of Savvy Auntie and author of *Otherhood*,
www.melanienotkin.com

Diane Pottinger, New York City celebrity makeup artist,
www.dianepottinger.com

Tonya Reiman, body language expert and author of *The Yes Factor*,
www.tonyareiman.com

Peter Shankman, customer service and marketing futurist and best-selling
author of *Zombie Loyalists: Using Great Service to Create Rabid Fans*,
www.shankman.com

Julie Spira, cyber dating expert and author of *The Perils Of Cyber Dating*,
www.cyberdatingexpert.com

Amanda Steinberg, founder of DailyWorth.com, www.dailyworth.com.

Jennifer Tuma-Young, wellness coach and author of *Balance the Scale,
Balance Your Life*, www.inspiredgirl.net

Steph L. Wagner, financial expert and divorce strategist, www.stephlwagner
.com

Kerri Zane, single-mom lifestyle expert and author of *It Takes All 5: A Single
Mom's Guide to Finding the REAL One*, www.kerrizane.com

Recommended Reading

I am a readaholic. I love books. I love the smell of them. I love the thought of them. And I love the fact that while I am learning, I am able to escape into another world. Whether I am working through a self-help book to encourage and inspire or a great novel, books are a part of who I am as I continue on this journey in life. From some oldies but goodies to some fun books to some books that helped me get through each day, I hope you find a few gems on this list that enrich your life like they have mine.

All Fall Down, Jennifer Weiner
Balance the Scale, Balance Your Life, Jennifer Tuma-Young
Crazy, Sexy, Diet, Kris Carr
Daring Greatly, Brene Brown
Eat What You Kill, Ted Scofield
Good in Bed, Jennifer Weiner
The Happiness Project, Gretchen Rubin
If the Buddha Dated, Charlotte Sophia Kasl
It Takes All 5: A Single Mom's Guide to Finding the Real One, Kerri Zane
Lean In, Sheryl Sandberg
Love in 90 Days, Dr. Diana Kirschner
Lucky Us, Amy Bloom
Otherhood, Melanie Notkin
The Paris Wife, Paula McLain
The Power Trip, Jackie Collins
Secrets of Longevity, Hundreds of Ways to Live to Be 100, Dr. Mao Shing Ni

Think, Lisa Bloom
Unstuff Your Life! Andrew Mellon
The Vacationers, Emma Straub
What I Know For Sure, Oprah Winfrey
Where We Belong, Emily Giffin
Why We Love, Helen Fisher
The Yes Factor, Tonya Reiman
You Can Heal Your Life, Louise L. Hay

References

(1) www.goop.com/journal/be/conscious-uncoupling

(2) www.wf-lawyers.net/divorce-statistics-and-facts/

(3) http://bmjopen.bmj.com/content/3/12/e004277.full?sid=f40b344f-ef24
-4a2d-9c09-59516f35fefc

(4) Source: Gary Taubes, Why We Get Fat and What to
Do About It, http://garytaubes.com/

(5) http://eatlocalgrown.com/article/12671-coconut-oil-evidence-based
-health-benefits.html

(6) www.plosone.org/article/info%3Adoi%2F10.1371%2Fjournal.pone
.0016268

(7) www.amazon.com/Act-Like-Lady-Think-Relationships/dp/0061728985

(8) www.amazon.com/Long-Walk-Freedom-Autobiography-Mandela/dp
/0316548189

(9) www.1043myfm.com/onair/valentine-in-the-morning-45207/idina
-menzel-talks-success-of-frozen-12492135/

(10) www.cbs.com/shows/the_talk/topics/show/1000863/

(11) http://ideas.time.com/2013/10/04/why-second-marriages-are-more
-perilous/

Index